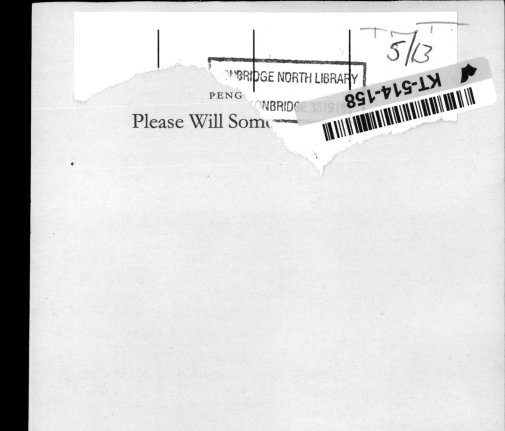

Please Will Someone Help Me?

*A mother who hated her, a grandfather who abused her,
and a system blind to what was going on*

BY SOPHIE YOUNG

with Linda Watson-Brown

PENGUIN BOOKS

PENGUIN BOOKS

Published by the Penguin Group
Penguin Books Ltd, 80 Strand, London WC2R ORL, England
Penguin Group (USA) Inc., 375 Hudson Street, New York, New York 10014, USA
Penguin Group (Canada), 90 Eglinton Avenue East, Suite 700, Toronto, Ontario, Canada M4P 2Y3
(a division of Pearson Penguin Canada Inc.)
Penguin Ireland, 25 St Stephen's Green, Dublin 2, Ireland (a division of Penguin Books Ltd)
Penguin Group (Australia), 707 Collins Street, Melbourne, Victoria 3008, Australia
(a division of Pearson Australia Group Pty Ltd)
Penguin Books India Pvt Ltd, 11 Community Centre, Panchsheel Park,
New Delhi – 110 017, India
Penguin Group (NZ), 67 Apollo Drive, Rosedale, Auckland 0632,
New Zealand (a division of Pearson New Zealand Ltd)
Penguin Books (South Africa) (Pty) Ltd, Block D, Rosebank Office Park, 181 Jan Smuts Avenue,
Parktown North, Gauteng, 2193, South Africa

Penguin Books Ltd, Registered Offices: 80 Strand, London WC2R ORL, England

www.penguin.com

First published in Penguin Books 2013
001

Copyright © Sophie Young, 2013
Linda Watson-Brown, 2013
All rights reserved

The moral right of the author has been asserted

Typeset in 12.5/14.75pt Garamond MT Std by Palimpsest Book Production Ltd,
Falkirk, Stirlingshire
Printed in Great Britain by Clays Ltd, St Ives plc

ISBN: 978-0-718-17737-9

www.greenpenguin.co.uk

Penguin Books is committed to a sustainable
future for our business, our readers and our planet.
This book is made from Forest Stewardship
Council™ certified paper.

ALWAYS LEARNING   **PEARSON**

For my husband – who has always been my rock

Contents

The chapters of this book are preceded by direct quotes from Sophie's social work files and relate to the many assessments made of her and her family over the years.

Prologue

I have an ordinary life.

Ordinary but wonderful.

Most days start the same way – there is a frenzy of breakfasts, wiping faces clean, teeth-brushing, then everyone heads off to work and school. When I start my first big tidy of the day the house is quiet of the usual noise, so I fill it up again with music. As I clean and dust and put things back in their place in the empty house, I sing along to songs and dance.

I've always loved music. It's been my saviour. Whenever things were bad – and they've been bad so many, many times – I've escaped into music. Whether listening out for snatches of a song on the radio, or filling my house with music when I get the chance, it's been there for me. Something to hold on to, something that never changes or turns on me.

The house is empty now, but that's rare. With five children, every day is busy. Each one passes in a blur of the usual everyday things – washing, cooking, dropping them off, picking them up, laughing, hugging, singing, being together. I adore them. I probably adore them more than they know because I want their childhoods to be straight-forward and uncomplicated; I don't want them to feel that I'm suffocating them with my love – but they are my world.

Daisy, the youngest, is a bundle of energy and delight. She's only six and she is my last baby, my only girl, the apple of everyone's eye. She looks so like me when I was that age; I feel as if I'm watching myself all those years ago.

As I clean up, I look at all their photos on the walls and shelves and mantelpiece. I can't get enough of gazing at them, and I sometimes can't believe that I've brought these perfect children into the world.

I could complain that the washing machine never seems to stop. The pile of ironing never seems to disappear. There are always dishes to be cleared, things to be taken upstairs, things to be brought downstairs, toys to tidy away, clothes to fold, drawers to close, beds to make – the list is endless, and I'm happy with it that way. If I keep busy, I can't think so much. If I don't think so much, I can pretend I'm always happy, and everything is always perfect.

It's very close to being that way, it really is. The children are wonderful; my husband is caring and loving. I have friends and I'm healthy. It would be nice to have a bit more money, to have something extra in our pockets at the end of the month, but there are more important things. So, I get through the days by concentrating on what matters – my family and my love for them.

The music continues to belt out from the speakers in my living room, and I have a vague awareness of other noises too. The bins are being emptied from the pavements outside my front window. Car doors are being slammed shut as other parents come back from school drop-offs. The gate squeaks open as the postman walks up the path.

The gate squeaks open as the postman walks up the path.

The gate squeaks open as the postman walks up the path.

It's like a moment in a film when you know something bad is going to happen but there's absolutely nothing you can do to stop it. It repeats in my head over and over, even although only a couple of seconds have passed. He's coming. The postman is coming. And, if he is, I know what he's bringing. My throat goes dry. I feel sick. My stomach lurches. I think I'm going to faint.

I turn the music up louder, but I still hear it. I still hear the doorbell and I know why he's ringing it. We rarely get interesting mail; it's unusual for there to be something that needs to be signed for. But I know that is exactly why he's ringing the bell today – I need to sign for something and I know what it is.

I take a deep breath and look at myself in the hall mirror just before I open the door.

'*You can do this,*' I whisper. '*You can do this.*'

I can say the words, but I'm not sure that I believe

them. I've coped with some terrible things in my life, and the fact that I'm opening the door to the postman shouldn't even register, but it's up there – it's up there with the most monumental things I've ever experienced.

I'm greeted by the words, 'Morning, love!' as soon as I open the door. The sun is shining and the world is going about its business, while mine is spinning. The postman has a big smile on his face and a large padded envelope in his hands. I can't take my eyes off it. I know what's in there. I've waited for it for such a long time, getting a knot in my stomach every morning when I've wondered if this was the day it would arrive, feeling relief when it hasn't and I've been given a pardon for another twenty-four hours.

'Sign here, my darling,' he says cheerily and I match his smile – I'm good at going through the motions. I can always paint the right happy look on my face even when I'm dying inside. I've had years of practice. As he passes the package over to me his words run through my bones and chill me.

'Hope it's something nice,' he says, winking.

I can't answer.

I know what it is – and it isn't something nice at all.

This package contains my social work records from over thirty years ago. Pages and pages of documents chronicling a little girl and her life. Pages and pages written by people who have, no doubt, long forgotten me, while I have yearned to know what they thought, how they made their decisions, and what they believed was going on behind closed doors.

I've wanted and dreaded this for so long – from before

the day when I made the official request, from before the day when I discovered that I could access every file ever written about me.

I look at the huge envelope in my hands and start to shake.

It's my past.

I'm holding my past.

Chapter 1

Always trouble

Sophie is a slim, dark-haired, attractive
child – she has had many responsibilities unusual
for her age and has an inappropriate knowledge of
the adult world.
Social work report on case number 4325 G/
Sophie Gilmore

Before I had my own children, I had very few happy
memories. One of the reasons I try to make every day
special for them is because no one ever did that for me.
There *must* have been happy times back when I was a little
girl – surely there must? Surely no one can live with every
day being full of misery and hate, of unpredictability and
anger? Sometimes I don't know; sometimes it seems that
all my head holds is memories that I would do anything to
get rid of.

I was born to a couple who had problems before I even
arrived on the scene. Like so many – too many – children,
I wasn't planned. I just happened, and that was the start
of it all. I never got the sense that my parents were madly

in love with each other, they never told me stories of how they fell head over heels, there were no funny tales of flirting or tentatively moving towards being a happy pair.

Dad was always controlling. If he wanted something, it didn't really matter what Mum said or did, he expected to get his own way. Mind you, saying that, she was no shrinking violet. From what I can piece together, she spent most of their time together shouting and kicking off – throughout it all he ignored it when she made her feelings known and the only way he ever responded was with his fists.

From the moment Ali and Jennifer became a couple, there seems to have always been an undercurrent of something unpleasant. Dad, even back then, laid down the rules of the relationship. Mum didn't seem to be bothered about getting away or ending it – she might have been loud and stroppy, but she stayed with him, which is something I could never quite fathom. Dad was very good-looking, and maybe the attraction was as superficial as that, but she was beautiful too and could have had her pick of the boys if only she had broken away from him. I guess if she had, I wouldn't be here today – sometimes I wish that was the case, I really do.

There was another aspect to their relationship that may have added a sense of being different or breaking the rules to a young couple in those days. Dad was black – and, despite it being a time when more and more immigrants were coming to the country, there was a huge amount of racism that both he and Mum faced every time they went out together. Maybe that made them feel that, like many other teenagers, they were fighting discrimination or paving a new way, though I never heard that was the case. I can only make assumptions, because all I know about what Mum felt regarding Dad's ethnicity was that it was something to use against me as I grew up.

When Mum was sixteen she left school and got a job on a packing line in a factory. I think, for a while, she was happy. She hadn't enjoyed school and wasn't academically inclined, so when she began work there was a sense of freedom in her life, but Dad was still there so the freedom was limited. I know that she did what she could to show her own personality within the confines of their relationship. She would wear mini skirts and bright colours, the fashion of the time, with her blonde hair piled high and flicked-out eyeliner that showed off her sparkling blue eyes. She did have some friends, but it seemed that nothing could stop the inevitability of her relationship with Ali. Within the first month of them sleeping together, Mum was pregnant. That was me – that was the auspicious start to my life. If there was love and passion, if there was a sense of destiny and adoration, I never heard about it.

So, I was born nine months later to a young couple who were clueless and had ended up together without ever thinking of the consequences. The parents on both sides were appalled. Dad's parents had very strong family values. They had expected him to marry a girl they approved of and who they had known for some time, as well as hoping she would be from the same ethnic background. They were horrified when they found out that he and Mum had been sleeping together before they were married. Although it was the early 1970s and most people

3

were enjoying more open relationships, there were too many taboos in this one for the older generation to accept it. Not only were Mum and Dad having sex when they were so young, and so unmarried, they weren't taking any precautions and they were forcing their families to face up to issues of race and ethnicity in a way that none of them were comfortable with. The racism around them got even worse when it looked as if white girls were being 'made pregnant' by 'foreigners'. Racism was everywhere. In my reports it states:

Sophie is half-cast [sic] . . . it is believed her father may even be black.

The comments are worded as if I was lower than other people because of my dual heritage. The reports simply reflect how many people felt, whether they were speaking in an official capacity or not. At that time, Mum and Dad lived in Manchester, which had played host to lots of immigrants, but that didn't necessarily make things better – in fact, it may have made things worse as people often felt threatened and challenged by incoming groups. My dad and his family were called names constantly, and it didn't matter whether any of the insults were accurate, the people around them saw anyone with a different skin colour as fair game. Dad would be called 'black' or 'darkie' or 'nigger' or 'Paki' or any one of a hundred other words that were just common speech back then, and it made no difference to the person hurling the insult whether he was actually from that ethnic group. It was all the same to them – he was an incomer and now he had committed

4

the ultimate sin of getting a white girl pregnant outside marriage.

Mum said that things were a bit different for her in that lots of her friends thought she had landed a real catch. Ali was dark and handsome, and the other teenage girls had romantic visions about their relationship, not knowing that it was far from dreamy. They saw him as different too, but in a good way, holding notions that he was going to sweep my mother away from their boring surroundings. The dreams of these girls could not have been further from the truth.

At the centre of it all, the very person who should have given unconditional support to Mum was furious. My maternal grandma, Grace, was livid. Not only was she horrified by her daughter getting pregnant out of wedlock at sixteen, but it was, as she put it, 'to a dirty darkie'. She didn't mince her words at the best of times, and racism was in her nature. She would be a granny in her early forties and she said that she'd be shamed by my birth. When Mum told her she was having a baby, after the initial insults and anger Grandma left the room. Mum sat on a chair, crying, full of hormones and confusion, wondering what to do. She hoped that her own mum would get her anger out while she was away and come back with a plan, a list of what she would do to make everything fine for her teenage daughter in her time of need.

Grandma returned about an hour later, telling her exhausted daughter, 'I'm going to run a bath for you. You'll get in, you won't complain about it being boiling hot, and you'll drink this.' She handed her a brown glass bottle, the sort you used to get medicine in. It had no labels or details, but she would have known its purpose even if Grandma hadn't said to her, 'We'll get that darkie bastard out of you one way or another.' Not all young women had benefited from the after-effects of the Swinging Sixties. They may have been having sex outside marriage, but emancipation soon disappeared when they found themselves pregnant. Young women like my mum, uneducated and working class, weren't always on the Pill, and sex was something that was still more for men than them. There were still back-street abortions even though the Abortion Act had been passed, and getting rid of an unwanted pregnancy could be lethal for a young woman who was willing to try anything. Equality soon went out of the window when you were a poor, unmarried teenager. It was still the case that many young women were considered to have loose morals if they 'allowed' a boy to have sex with them without a ring on their finger. Despite all the talk of female equality and feminism, it was just that – 'talk' – for millions. Women who got pregnant outside marriage, and who were working class and in a dual-heritage relationship like my mum, were either sluts or victims. Mum had admitted to Grandma that she had been willing, that Ali hadn't forced her, which meant that she fell into the slut category – and Grandma saw aborting me as the only solution.

I don't get a sense that my grandparents had big plans for my mum. They weren't horrified that she was pregnant with me because it would stop her going to university or following a big career, they just didn't want the neighbours talking, and they certainly didn't want a 'black' grandchild. I have no idea where my grandfather, Arthur, was when all this was being dealt with. I suspect that it would still have been seen as women's business, and he would have kept well away from the matter, taking an out of sight, out of mind approach.

Mum refused to drink what Grandma provided her, or to get in the boiling-hot bath, so her own mother told her to leave the house. Mum packed what few possessions she had and moved into the flat Dad already had in the centre of Manchester, hoping for a softening in her mother's attitude. It didn't come – Grace felt that her daughter had disgraced her, and she would not even speak to her while she carried me.

Mum didn't give in. She didn't have an abortion, despite many people trying to persuade her it would be for the best, and she waited for the next six months to pass. There was little support or money, so the young parents-to-be moved to Liverpool, where my paternal grandma and granddad lived. They were very traditional and viewed Mum in much the same way as her own mother had: as a slut who had trapped their good boy of a son. This set of grandparents had wanted so much for their son. They had come to this country in search of a better life and they saw the way to that as being through hard work and education. My dad had already disappointed them. Dad hadn't taken advantage of the many opportunities they thought were perfect for him in Britain. They had hoped that he would do well at school, go on to university, become a doctor or lawyer or engineer, before eventually settling down with a girl they approved of and beginning his family life in his own home, with a good salary and a shining future. None of that had looked like a possibility before Mum came on to the scene because Dad was lazy and volatile. However, the arrival of a sixteen-year-old English girl who seemed to have no morals and who had got pregnant practically the first time she'd had sex with their son made things so much worse. My paternal grandparents never made any attempt to build a relationship with Mum, and blamed her for everything in Dad's life from that point on.

With no parental support, Dad had persuaded Mum that moving to Liverpool would offer them a chance to start afresh. No one would know them there and they could raise their baby without others passing judgement. It wasn't to be. Mum hated Liverpool just as much as she'd hated Manchester, and when they married with no ceremony or fuss she felt let down even more. The young couple got a horrible flat in a rough part of town, and with few possessions or money settled into their new life together. When I got older, Mum told me that this is when things changed between her and her new husband. During her pregnancy, Dad had been a million miles from any notion of an attentive father-to-be. He made friends easily in Liverpool, but he also had the life of a young, single man. He would drink and gamble, he would stay out all night, there were rumours that he was with other women. As he continued his life just as he had before, Mum sat in the flat, getting bigger with a pregnancy she was no longer sure she wanted. There were times when she wondered whether she should have gone along with her mother's wishes after all.

When Dad did come back, she'd shout and rant at

him. He would then remember that he had responsibilities and would blame his new wife for everything. He started hitting her, punching her without any consideration for the fact that she was pregnant, and not even caring if he left bruises or other marks. Mum didn't really go anywhere or see anyone, so perhaps he reasoned that he would get away with it. He did. Mum never reported him and I was born, perfect, on time and with little bother.

Mum never told me any stories of the day I was born. There were never any warm cuddles on a sofa while she talked about my first cry or the smell of me when I was a newborn; there were no happy memories of that day as far as I could tell. I know that I was born in a hospital, not in the flat, and I know that Dad got there much later that evening. I guess that was another opportunity missed. They could have been reconciled. They could have decided to make a fresh start. It never happened.

I think the way Mum saw it was simple – she was pregnant, her life was ruined, then she had me and things got even worse.

Exhausted with caring for a newborn, Mum wouldn't keep quiet about how unhappy she was. My dad was from a traditional background and believed that women were there to look after children in an uncomplaining fashion, just as his mother and all the women in his family had done. He didn't take kindly to his young wife's words – and he responded with his fists.

The relationship had been unhealthy from the start. He was always controlling. Mum had just turned seventeen when she had me. By all accounts, I was a beautiful baby.

I was cooed over wherever she went as I had inherited many of Dad's features, with my thick black hair and huge brown eyes. If she took me out without Dad she got a lot of attention; she was a lovely looking young girl herself and I was a cute newborn, but when Dad was there it was a different story because of his skin colour. I hadn't inherited that, I only looked lightly tanned really, but when the mixed-race young couple were out and about with their little girl, the racism of the early 1970s kicked in hard.

It must have been so difficult for Mum, and I do sympathize. She was no more than a child herself: seventeen years old, just married to a man who had changed his character, estranged from her own family, and caring for a baby she had never planned. It was a lot to carry, and now she was paying for it.

Dad was unpredictable. His anger and violence could come from nothing, and he was very open about it. Unlike a lot of wife beaters, he didn't seem to think through what he was doing. He didn't always hit her in the stomach or somewhere else that was hidden; he would hit her where and when he liked, even if it meant that the bruises were clearly visible. No one appeared to challenge him on it. He got away with everything, which meant that he never had to change his ways. Mum was just his property: the slag of a white girl who had fallen into bed with him, having unprotected sex without a ring on her finger. He had no respect for her, and showed that by beating her senseless whenever the mood took him.

One day, when I was just a little baby, she was carrying me around the flat when he kicked off. He lifted up some metal baby reins that were lying nearby – my mum used to buy things from charity shops whenever she saw them as there was so little money and this was one of her most recent buys even though I was a long way off walking – and wrapped them round his hands. He walked towards her, aiming the metal buckles at her – and me. She turned to the wall to protect me and he split her head open with them.

I think, back then, she did try to look after me in her own way. She took me everywhere with her, and seemed to revel in people telling her what a beautiful baby I was. In those early years I loved her so much and she loved me so much that I couldn't bear to be apart from her. I didn't even walk until I was two because she carried me all the time.

Grandma Grace had started speaking to Mum again once she saw me. The granddaughter she thought she would hate, who she had wanted to abort, became the apple of her eye. She cooed over me and bought me things, showed me off proudly to other women her age who, it turned out, were more interested in gurgling over a little one than gossiping about the colour of her dad's skin.

We got a council house after a little while, but things were still bad and Dad was still hitting Mum. I can't remember a time when there wasn't shouting and scream-ing in our house. There was always an atmosphere of violence, either already happening or about to erupt at any second.

One summer afternoon, Dad asked Mum to go to the local shops for him. This was something he always did, because he hated having to interact with people unless he absolutely had to, whereas it didn't bother Mum too much as she could cope with any insults or catcalls. She left me in my baby bouncer in front of the washing machine and switched a load on before she left, knowing that I loved the noise and watching the clothes swirl round.

When she came back, I was screaming.

Mum picked me up, and I had red marks all over me.

'What have you done?' she furiously asked my dad.

He was standing at the sink, shaving, as if he didn't have a care in the world. Mum kept nudging him to get his attention, but he was acting as if she wasn't even there. Eventually, he shrugged.

'She was screaming for you and it was doing my head in. I rolled up a newspaper and gave her a few whacks. Didn't shut her up, though.'

He was shameless about his violence. It's hard to know what age you are when things happen in those early years, but I have clear memories of not being able to walk – so I must have been under two – and always watching, looking to see how things were between them. The interaction was always so quick; they reacted in a millisecond to each other so if one of them kicked off it would escalate immediately. There never seemed to be a time when it would calm down; neither of them had the ability to defuse a situation, and they would wind the other up constantly. Of course, there is no justification for my dad's violence, and even if Mum had managed to calm him down he would probably still have hit her, but I quickly became used to everything flaring up in what seemed a moment and then becoming fast and scary almost immediately.

I learned to watch as much as I learned to listen. Mum would always say I was nosey, but I was just trying to predict the mood. When they were fighting I would look from one to the other, trying desperately to understand the body language between them. Often, when Dad was hitting Mum she would look at me, her eyes pleading with me – but what *could* I do? When they talked, I sat and watched. When they fought, I sat and watched. I was soaking it all up, looking for signs of it escalating.

Although it was hard living in the middle of all that violence, I didn't know anything else. I idolized my mum; she was so pretty, I wanted to be with her all the time – and I was, but I don't remember many cuddles, even back when it was all fine between us.

Despite everything that had gone on between my mum and her own mother, she was missing Grandma Grace, who wouldn't travel to us when Dad was there. Grandma did drive, so it was possible for her to visit, but she would only do so if her son-in-law was out and Mum resented this; she wanted her mother round for company and to help her in the lonely life she had made for herself.

However, and conveniently for Grandma, Dad was always disappearing. He was never a constant presence at home, and it was during one of his disappearing acts that Mum left Liverpool and headed back to Manchester. She moved both of us into a bed and breakfast just before I was two without warning her husband. She couldn't have thought he wouldn't react, it wasn't in his nature – and, I suspect, she was just as bad as him and knew no other way to maintain the relationship other than the constant drama they were both used to and were expert at provoking.

It wasn't long before Dad did reappear and moved back in after tracking us down, then the shouting and constant violence started again. Whether I was asleep or awake, the only backdrop was shouting and screaming. It was the soundtrack of my childhood. I was a restless, unsettled child as a result, because I could never relax, but Mum did love me and she continued to keep me with her all the time.

After our move, Dad seemed to be around a bit more. Things settled for a little while – Mum was acting like a mum, she was nurturing and attentive when she could be bothered, and my maternal grandparents were now in my life too. I started walking round about then, which meant that she wasn't having to carry me everywhere. As the mother of five children, I've often thought about this. Two years old is pretty late for a child to begin walking if they have no physical problems. I actually think that I made a conscious decision *not* to walk; if I couldn't do it, then Mum had to carry me, she had to keep me close to her, she had to continue that contact. I was a tiny little girl living in a domestic war zone. I never knew when it would erupt, and no matter how much I looked for the signs they could always catch me unawares. By refusing to walk, by refusing to physically remove myself from my mother, I was ensuring that some degree of closeness *had* to be maintained. I can also only assume that once we moved to the house in Manchester and things calmed down for a while, I felt secure enough to make the break and start walking on my own.

There were more changes going on in my life at that point. My little sister, Fiona, was born when I was three. I was too young to notice that Mum's tummy was getting bigger and no one told me anything about what was happening. There was no build-up to the baby coming, but I suppose that, with Dad's temper and violence, Mum would probably never have allowed herself to let her guard down for a second throughout the pregnancy. He had already kicked at least one baby out of her, and she would go on to have more miscarriages caused by him and abortions at his command. I don't know how many pregnancies she went through to have me and my two younger brothers, but I think, even with Fiona, she wouldn't have let herself feel a pregnancy would necessarily end with a baby after nine months.

My little sister wasn't with us for long. One morning, Mum went over to the cot to pick her up and Fiona had died. My baby sister was a silent victim of cot death.

To lose a child in such a way is always a terrible tragedy. Cot death rips families apart and I know that those who suffer as a result of it spend the rest of their lives wondering why it happened, what they could have done to prevent it, how they can wind the clock back. Mum was no different and it broke her heart to lift the tiny cold body of her baby from the cot that morning. For a woman who spent most of her days screaming and wailing, she was uncharacteristically quiet. Nothing could accurately show how much agony she was in, so she said nothing. She said nothing when the doctor came and confirmed Fiona was dead. She said nothing when the undertakers came to remove her tiny little body. She said nothing as her baby was buried.

I think that was it.

I think that was when a little bit of Mum gave up.

She had always found life difficult, she had always felt

hard done by in her relationship, and now she had lost a baby, a part of herself.

But the day that Fiona died, I didn't just lose my little sister. I lost my childhood. Things would never be the same again.

Chapter 2

Why are you here?

Sophie is clearly a disturbed little girl who requires
a respite from her home situation and the domestic
friction there, a setting where she can receive
consistent care and control that is appropriate.
Social work report 4325G/
Sophie Gilmore

Dad had been controlling towards Mum since the start of
their relationship, but now the violence seemed to happen
every day and the home situation was appalling, unpredictable and brutal. I feel that I never really had a
relationship with him because I could never tell when his
temper was going to erupt. He wasn't like a dad; he was
just this scary man who sometimes lived with us and
always hit my mum when he was around.

All I wanted was her really. I was desperate for her love.
I just wanted to be with her all the time. I did despise my
dad when he was horrible to her; I couldn't understand
how he could do it, how he could hit the person I loved so
much.

Not only was I always scared, I was also a desperately shy child. Whenever anyone came to the door, I would hide under Mum's skirt; I just wanted it to be the two of us. To be honest, it usually was. I remember Dad leaving a lot, but I don't really recall all the times he came back – and, yet, he *did* come back. He never stayed away permanently. He'd be away for weeks on end and I noticed his absences even more when Fiona died. I have no idea whether that's because I was getting older and was more aware anyway, or whether the death of my little sister had been the final nail in their relationship. I never saw my parents comfort each other after their second daughter died. I wasn't at the funeral, I can't remember who looked after me that day, but even though I was small I would have been aware of a change in my home atmosphere. I would have noticed if they had been loving towards one another, or helped each other through their grief. The sad fact is their relationship didn't change. They didn't suddenly see that life was too short and that they should be kinder, they didn't suddenly act as a proper family with the child who remained, they just kept shouting and hitting and hating.

It was at this time that Mum started changing. As a mother myself, I can only imagine the horror of losing a child to cot death. I love my own kids with every part of me, and I know that if any of them had died as a baby, I would have been broken into a million pieces. Mum wasn't one to show her emotions in that sense. She rarely cried and I wonder whether that was because, as a woman who had been beaten so often and so heartlessly by the man she should have loved and who should have loved her, she had trained herself not to. Perhaps it angered my dad still further, perhaps it made him beat her even more, or perhaps she didn't want to give him the satisfaction of seeing just how much he had hurt her. Whatever the reason, she wasn't the type of person to burst into tears; losing her baby would have been more than enough justification to finally show that side of her, but maybe it had been closed off for so long that she didn't know how to let it loose again. I only know that she was hit hard by Fiona's death, not because she told me but because I actually witnessed it.

From that tender age, when I was only three, I was set up in direct competition with the baby sister who had died. I had adored my mum before Fiona left us – I still did – and I had spent so much time with her, but she changed, almost overnight, into a hard, cruel person who would look at me as if she couldn't quite work out what I was doing there.

'Why her?' she would ask me.

I was only a little girl, and I'd usually be playing with the very few toys I had (there weren't many around as we never had spare cash) when she would start to ask me these bizarre questions.

'Why did Fiona die and not you?' she'd wonder aloud.

It went on and on.

Why have I been left with you?

Why are you here but she's been taken from me?

What did I do to lose her but get saddled with you?

Why are you still here but she's gone?

I couldn't answer any of it, of course, and I don't think she wanted me to – she just needed to vent and to get her loss out in some way. I guess it was unfortunate – more than unfortunate – that she chose a three-year-old child who adored her to bear the brunt of it all. I do think it's perfectly understandable for any parent who has lost a child to ask these questions in order to begin to deal with the terrible sadness and anger they feel and question why their baby has gone – but that shouldn't mean asking a little child why they survived instead of their sibling, making it so very clear that they think this is a terrible thing. No one could feel anything but pity for a mother or father who has lost a baby to cot death, but Mum's reaction and her taking it out on me was not normal in any way.

We lived in a rough area in not very nice accommodation, but after Fiona passed Mum started cleaning all the time. I didn't know what the appropriate label was in those days, but I do now – she had obsessive-compulsive disorder, OCD, and with little warning she was soon in the grip of it. It was as if she turned into a cleaning machine overnight. She'd get up at the crack of dawn and start cleaning, then sleep for the rest of the day. When she woke, she'd start all over again: dusting, vacuuming, washing, sweeping, wiping. Soon the neighbours were complaining as she seemed to have no concept of time when she was in the throes of it; it could be the middle of the night or first thing in the morning, but still she would have the Hoover on or be clattering things about.

This was the beginning of real problems with the people who lived around us. They had moaned a bit in the past about the noise when my parents were kicking off, but most people stay out of 'domestics' even when the victim is being kicked to hell and back. From what my grandma told me in later years, they cut Mum a bit of slack after Fiona's death, but soon the noise at all hours simply became too much. She gave them short shrift. Sometimes she'd open the door to tell them to 'fuck off', or sometimes she would simply shout it above the noise she was making.

The other thing Mum started to do was develop weird little patterns and habits. Before Fiona had died, she would simply lift me up and we'd head out for shopping or a trip to Grandma's house; now she had lots of rituals to go through. She'd check locks, straighten furniture, move things an inch, move them back again, straighten the same furniture, wipe a light switch with a cloth, fold the cloth in a particular way, look at the cloth, refold it. And, all the time, she would be muttering to herself, saying the same words over and over again, words that I couldn't quite catch but which seemed important to her. If I interrupted, sometimes only to ask what she was saying, she'd tell me to shut my stupid mouth and she'd begin the process again.

It made no sense to me but it seemed to be what she needed to do for her own peace of mind. Although, actually, saying that, I'm not too sure she ever *had* any peace of mind. Even when she did all the things she needed to do, even when she cleaned and positioned and chanted, she wasn't happy. I don't mean happy in a way that would have been impossible for any woman who had just lost a child, but happy in a settled way that would allow her even to grieve normally. I never saw her cry or mourn for Fiona in a healthy way, and I think that the quick onset of OCD was one of the clearest signs that

Mum went through some sort of awful mental breakdown.

Her behaviour also changed in that she started getting boyfriends who would come to the house regularly when Dad was away. Mum was really pretty at that time. When she was horrid to me her face contorted into something terrible and she lost her looks, but superficially she was a striking-looking woman. She was still very young, barely twenty, and had long blonde hair, which was never dyed but a natural honey colour that matched her big blue eyes perfectly. She was always trim with a figure that belied the fact that she had already been through two full-term pregnancies, and she could put on a good show, laughing and joking as if that was her personality, giving men attention and ensuring that they felt well looked after. Those men didn't tend to stay around for long, but if they were there a few times, they often introduced themselves to me. There was a procession of 'uncles' who would bend down to me as I sat playing, tell me that they were pleased to meet me, urge me to be a good girl for a bit, then disappear into the bedroom with my mum for a while.

I would hear strange noises coming from there, noises that I couldn't understand, but they didn't seem to be the kind of noises Mum and Dad made when they were fighting, so I wasn't too worried. Sometimes I would even hear Mum giggling. She didn't laugh much, and it never appeared natural, but when one of the uncles seemed to want that reaction, she could do it.

I was often left on my own to play when these men came round, and I would also be hurried off to my room at all hours of the day and night to give them 'a bit of peace'. Sometimes I would tell Mum that I would be quiet if she let me stay with her, but she'd get up from the sofa where she was hugging an uncle, hurriedly push me out of the room, and hiss at me, 'Oh, just fuck off out of my sight – I can't believe you're still fucking here, so don't give me another reason to hate you.'

I remember one night, as I was getting ready for bed, Mum was sitting on the settee as usual with a new uncle. She'd told me to get my nightdress on, but, as I went toddling off, the uncle said, 'Has she had her bath yet?'

'No, she'll be fine,' Mum answered. 'Hurry up, Sophie – get yourself off to bed and leave us alone.'

The next thing I remember is that the uncle was in my bedroom with me as I got ready.

'Right – let's get you in the bath,' he said.

'She doesn't need a bath; she just needs to get to bloody sleep!' shouted Mum from the living room.

'No bother, no bother,' said the man, hurrying me through to the bathroom. I could hear Mum in the kitchen, probably filling up more glasses of wine, as I was saying that I didn't want a bath.

'I don't want you to bath me,' I said. 'Mum!' I called. 'Mum! I want you to bath me.'

He hushed me, saying, 'You'll be all right, you'll be all right.'

I remember feeling very uncomfortable as he put me in the bath and started to wash me as I continued to protest. The uncle helped me get into the bath and I still recall feeling very unsettled as he washed me. Did he touch me? Did he do anything untoward? I honestly don't know –

but what sticks in my mind is that I was clear about not wanting this to happen and my wishes didn't carry any weight whatsoever. Mum just ignored me. It wasn't that she was actively pushing for this stranger to bathe me; it was that she was perfectly happy to go along with it for an easy life. She wanted to have a drink and have some time with him – he wanted to give me a bath, so she let him do that in order to give him what he wanted, and, presumably, get what she wanted as a result.

That uncle was around a lot, but Dad would come back after a while, and whoever was my mum's boyfriend would then go away. I don't remember them ever reappearing; a new one would just turn up the next time.

Whenever Dad returned, it would all slot into place again. Dad always had plenty of female attention with his dark hair, dark eyes and muscular build. On the rare occasions when he took me out there would often be women talking to him, and it seemed to me that he knew them already. In fact, he would often wait in certain places until one of them arrived as if it had been planned. Neither he nor Mum ever said to me that I should keep quiet to the other parent about the assignations they had. I have no idea whether they had an open relationship or whether they simply didn't care what the other thought of them. Maybe the marriage was already too far gone, too broken, by that point for them to even pretend they were faithful to each other.

When Dad was back he'd watch cricket or wrestling on television – that was what took all his time up really. He didn't work much or do anything productive. I would hear Mum shouting at him if he 'lost' another job, and I would wonder where he had put it. She would scream that his 'bloody temperament' would have us all in the Poor House, wherever that was, and they'd fight for hours, before he'd plonk himself down in front of the telly again once she'd worn herself out with screaming.

I was always frightened to walk in front of the TV when he was watching something as he would shout at me if I got in his line of vision. I remember working out that if I crawled on my hands and knees to get something I wanted, then I could avoid his anger. He was really pleased when I started doing that and praised me, patting me on the back and saying I was a 'good girl'. But the situation was always volatile. He was horrible to Mum, and she was horrible to him as well. A lot of it happened while I was in bed, and I would hear it all kicking off. I'd tentatively creep out of my bedroom, go into theirs, and generally see some evidence of Dad's violence to Mum. She'd have the start of bruises or a black eye, she'd have blood on her or be upset. My reports state:

Sophie describes him as a violent man . . . she said he is continually starting trouble in the house, accusing her mother of going out with other men.
   Social work files on 4325G/
   Sophie Gilmore

So, the reports do suggest that there were often fights initiated because of the affairs – certainly those on Mum's side – but I know that they were long past caring about whether the other person was sleeping with someone else,

25

and that it was just an excuse for the fists to fly yet again. The terrible thing is that this was just my life. I didn't know anything else. That was normality for me.

I would sometimes say, 'Mummy, what's wrong?', but she'd just reply that she was fine, and tell me to get out of the room. Of course, I knew that she wasn't fine because she would be crying, but I also knew that I shouldn't hang around if I was told to go. I would look at her, know that she was upset, see that she was bruised, but I would also be confused about what was going on. To live in such an atmosphere of horrific and constant domestic abuse is frustrating and perplexing for any young child, but, on top of that, I was having to try to work out why Mum just wasn't the same any more.

When Dad was away I still spent a lot of time with her, but she definitely didn't seem to be the way she was before she'd had Fiona. To begin with, she became quite distant in that she left me to my own devices and paid little attention to me, but then she started to tell me off a lot, would get angry very easily and would say such nasty, nasty things.

'Why are you still here?' she'd hiss at me.

At first, I didn't know what she meant. Where was I meant to be? I was only three – where could I go without my mum?

'Why? Why are you still here? Why you?' she'd continue.

I couldn't respond, and that seemed to anger her even more.

'For Christ's sake!' she'd shout at me, putting her face close to mine. 'Why the fuck have I been left with you?

Why are you the one that's still here? Why did Fiona die and yet I've been left with you?'

I could only take these words in to a certain extent. At three, I understood how furious she was, and I understood that she didn't seem to like me any more, but I certainly couldn't understand why she was always wondering aloud why I was there and yet my baby sister was gone. I knew Fiona had died, but I was too little to process the loss of her. She hadn't been with us for long, so I hadn't formed any sort of bond, and yet I was constantly being compared to her and I couldn't work out how I was meant to answer Mum when she asked these things.

I didn't *know* why I was still there. I didn't *know* why Fiona was dead and I was still alive. I think Mum had turned completely in on herself. Instead of grieving and crying, she showed anger instead. She kept everything inside her and I bore the brunt. I felt as if I could never do anything right. I started to feel frightened of her, which had never happened before; in fact, in the past she had been my sanctuary, she had been the one who had kept me safe when Dad was at his most violent.

My life was completely erratic. I never knew when my father would be there or when he would be away. When he was at home, he hit Mum a lot and they argued constantly. There was no one else around to care for me. I didn't go to nursery – I suspect neither of my parents were ever organized enough for that to be set up. Despite Mum moving back to Manchester so that she could have contact with her own mother, there seemed to be very little of that, and my dad's parents were out of the picture completely. I didn't have aunties and uncles around (apart from the fake uncles), and there was no extended family to give me love or security. On top of that, Mum was changing. I couldn't work out what she wanted from me; all I knew was that she constantly asked why I was there when Fiona had been taken from her.

Into that world, when I was four, came another baby. My brother, Mark, was born with no ceremony. Mum hadn't told me that another baby was coming, and I don't remember noticing. I can only think that after Fiona's death she was very worried about the pregnancy and perhaps didn't dare to hope that she would have another baby. Whatever the reason, Dad had come back, they'd had one of their reconciliations (which never lasted for long), and Mark arrived nine months later. God only knows how many times my father had been there and then gone during those nine months, but he was there for a while when his son arrived.

Mark's arrival didn't make Mum any softer. One day, while I was looking at the baby in his pram, she came over and shoved me aside.

'Oh, I bloody wish it had been you that had died instead of your sister,' she hissed. 'I'm bloody sick of you – bugger off and stop bothering him.'

I hadn't been bothering Mark at all, I was just intrigued by him given that I was at the age when babies seemed lovely. I stood there, not quite sure what to do.

'Piss off!' Mum snapped. 'Do you know what? You were like this with Fiona, always *at* her, always . . . always poking her eyes. Do you remember that? Do you? Poking her eyes. Poke, poke, poke.'

I didn't remember it at all. Why was she trying to make me feel bad, I wondered. I barely recalled Fiona ever being there, and now it was as if Mum wasn't content with just saying she wished I was dead, she was also trying to make me feel guilty that I had done something to my baby sister. Maybe I had touched her, maybe I'd tried to cuddle her; I'm sure I would have been drawn to her, but Mum, as always, had to turn memories into hard, nasty things that would leave me feeling even worse.

I loved my little brother and no matter how many times Mum would tell me that she was 'bloody sick' of me and that I was 'nothing but trouble', I'd still creep into her room to give Mark a little kiss and cuddle when she wasn't looking. To this day, I can still get upset when I remember just how much I cared for him. I also had a feeling that I needed to protect him from everything that was going on. He was so little and so vulnerable that there were times I didn't see how he could survive in that house. I had a little girl's blind belief that she can be bigger and stronger and braver for her younger siblings, that she can look after them better than anyone in the world – and I used to make promises to myself that I would look after baby Mark as well as I could.

Dad didn't take to Mark at all. He would constantly taunt Mum that the baby wasn't his, that he was someone else's 'bastard', and this made me feel even more protective towards him. It seemed clear to me that Mark was my real baby brother and that we did have the same Dad, because we all looked alike (nothing like Mum but very like Dad, although our skin wasn't as dark), but this cut no ice and the 'bastard' jibes continued whenever

Dad saw Mark in Mum's arms. Mum, for her part, adored her boy. 'I always wanted a boy,' she'd say to him when I was in earshot, 'I always wanted a boy.' This made me even more confused; I thought it was Fiona she had wanted, but Fiona was a girl. If she had 'always' wanted a boy, but loved Fiona so much, the only conclusion I could reach was that it was *me* who was unlovable, *me* who she just didn't feel like a mother towards. I definitely felt even more unwanted when Mark came along, but it never affected how I felt about the baby, it made me even sadder that there must be something wrong with me. Looking at how Mum was with him, I could see that she was capable of love. She smiled when she was with him, she played and laughed. She hugged him and kissed him and told him he was a good boy, her special boy, but I got none of that. If she had been the same way with Mark as she was with me, it would have shown me that she just wasn't very good at being a mummy, but I could see otherwise. She was *very* good at being a mummy when she had a good child, a child who she could open her heart to. I wasn't that child. She wished Fiona was here and I was dead, and now she was able to show me how lovely she could be if I wasn't the horrible, hateful little girl she screamed at all the time. I yearned for just a little scrap of that love, but it was further out of my reach every single day.

I would hold Mark's hand whenever I could. I would soothe him when Dad was shouting, and, as he got older, I would hold him to me when it all kicked off between our parents. I'd tell him everything would be all right, even when I didn't believe my own words. It was hard, but I tried to be strong for him. I'd had no one looking out for me, but I swore that it wouldn't be like that for Mark – he had someone who loved him, he had his big sister, and I would fight for him as much as I could.

Chapter 3

My grandma

Her assumed 'adult' role within her family has
hindered any opportunities for normal progression
through childhood. She admits that her mother is
highly dependent on her.
Social work records 4325G/
Sophie Gilmore

Even a four-year-old can feel stress, no matter how strong
she's trying to be, and the effect of living in that sort of
environment was taking its toll. My sister had died, a new
baby had come into the family, my dad was in and out of
my life, Mum had changed and was saying hateful things
to me all the time, there was an atmosphere of unpredictability and violence, strange men were in our house when
Dad wasn't there – it was far from the perfect lifestyle for
any child. I had started to wet myself a lot, no doubt
because of how I was living, and it absolutely infuriated
Mum.

She'd scream at me when she came into my room and
realized it had happened again. She would tell me that I

was 'filthy', that I 'disgusted' her. She'd refuse to wash my sheets sometimes, saying that I needed to get used to living in my own mess, so, on those days, I would smell of stale urine all day and, at night, I would crawl back into my soiled bed knowing, just knowing, that it would happen again. The fact that Mum's OCD was still a large part of all our lives obviously meant that my bedwetting was even more annoying for her. There were already social workers involved with our family. We lived on a notorious estate and we regularly had the police at the door for the noises of violence coming from the house or for the fact that Mum cleaned at all hours of the day and night. I think it says a lot that the neighbours did report us. On estates like that, there is often a natural antipathy towards getting the 'authorities' involved and the police are rarely seen as supportive, but people must have been at their wits' end. I was used to seeing a policeman or woman sitting on our sofa. They'd usually smile at me as they spoke to Mum – it was generally Mum who dealt with them – and sometimes they'd seem really nice. If Mum was in a good mood, or a manipulative one, she'd make them a cup of tea, but there were times when she'd just give them a mouthful straight away, as she did with the neighbours. Whatever her response when they were there, her attitude when they left was always the same: 'Bastards,' she'd hiss. 'Never tell those fucking bastards anything, do you hear me? Never say a word to them that they can use against you, never tell them anything, never offer any information. They'll twist every fucking thing you say, you mark my words.'

Sometimes I would venture that they seemed nice, and Mum would launch into another of her set speeches.

'Nice? Nice? They'll have you in a fucking home before you know it given half the chance! Do you want that? Do you want to be taken away?'

Yes, sometimes I did. I couldn't understand why Mum wouldn't want rid of me too, given how she was with me, but she soon answered my unspoken query.

'And if they take you, they take Mark. I'm not having that, so keep your mouth shut, smile and tell them you're living in the middle of a fucking fairy tale,' she'd conclude. I don't actually remember them asking me much, as it happens, nor do I recall much in-depth questioning from the social workers who started to come round. Many of the reports from those early years are missing from my files, so I don't know what conclusions were reached; I can only assume that the professionals, the people who knew what they were doing, thought that my home life was absolutely fine and that the best thing for me was to keep me in an environment of hatred, cruelty and violence. A fucking fairy tale indeed.

By the time I was five I knew that I was vulnerable, even though I wouldn't have known what the word meant. I just wanted to be loved; I wanted to be loved by Mum more than anything. It didn't matter what she did or what she said to me, I ached for her. She had never once told me that she loved me. I started looking around, to see if this was how mums were. Maybe they all got cross, maybe they all said nasty things, maybe none of them loved girls, maybe they all only wanted boys or the babies they'd lost. I was constantly watching other little girls with their mummies and I soon realized that I was the unusual one. The other girls got cuddles even when they were walking along the street. If they were naughty by running too far ahead or playing in some dirt, their mummies would be cross for a little moment, then give them a hug before they went on their way, smiling and holding hands. The other mummies were always looking to see if their little girls were safe, making sure they weren't too close to the road or far from their sides. All I got was Mum shouting at me to 'move myself' whenever she did remember to check I was still there as she walked ahead with Mark in his pram.

I suppose a part of me had wanted to see other girls being treated as badly as I was because that, at least, would show that it was normal. Once I started watching, once I started seeing that wasn't how the world worked, I felt even more alone. I just wanted someone to help me; I just wanted someone to care.

As a result, I was always, always, always wanting to be someone else, anyone else, rather than me. That's never changed. I didn't like my life, and I felt like I was the piece of shit that Mum said I was. I knew it wasn't Mum's fault; she had just been unlucky enough to get landed with me. If I could change, if I was better, if I was a good little girl, then she would be able to love me like other mummies loved their daughters – but she couldn't, because of how I was. The problem was that I couldn't see what exactly it was that I had to change to make her like me more. I knew that I was 'trouble', that I was 'disgusting' for wetting the bed, but I couldn't see a way out, a way to make me a nice Sophie that she would like. There was definitely something about me that wasn't what she wanted.

Mum had also started hurling racially abusive insults at

me – it didn't matter that they were inaccurate. I would frequently be called a 'little Paki' just as much as I would be shouted at as a 'little nigger'. I guess that was her way of hating the part of me that was my dad, but it still hurt as it was yet another thing I couldn't change. She never said those words to Mark.

I felt as if I didn't belong, but there was one little ray of sunshine that had come into my life so slowly that I almost didn't notice it at first. Mum had fallen out with my grandma when she first discovered she was pregnant with me, and when she moved back to Manchester the relationship was still a little strained. However, they did see each other and there were attempts made at being civil. I think that once Grandma got to know me and Mark, things got a lot better. She was a good grandma to us, and she was the first person in my life who showed me real love. With Mum, I always hoped that she'd turn round one day and say, 'Sophie – I made a mistake; you're a special little girl and I love you so much.' It never happened, but Grandma *did* tell me that I was special and she *did* show me love.

I loved everything about her. I loved how she looked and how she smelled. I loved that she had a big house that was clean but not obsessively so. If I wanted to draw a picture at Grandma's, that was fine, I didn't get bawled at for making a mess. If I wanted a snack, that was fine too – there was always food and crumbs didn't matter. I could be a child there and my heart lifted with each visit. The other thing that was fantastic about Grandma's house was that she was always cooking nice things, and she had sweets. Mum cooked very rarely; we usually ate takeaways or stuff from tins, and she never gave me sweets, whereas Grandma liked to make sure she was feeding me and spoiling me with little things all the time. Spoiling didn't seem to be a bad thing in that house. But when Mum said the word, it always sounded hard and bad. If she saw Grandma slip me another chocolate bar, she'd try to grab it back, hissing that her mother was 'spoiling' me and turning me into a brat. Grandma Grace would just laugh and either take the chocolate back and give it to me with a smile, or get another one from the big jar on the kitchen shelf while Mum guzzled what she'd taken from me, as if she couldn't even bear for me to have that little pleasure.

If Granddad saw me get sweets or chocolate, he'd be much nicer about it.

'Oooh, you're getting spoiled by your grandma, aren't you?' He'd smile, in a kindly way, tickling me under the chin. 'Our little Sophie loves her sweets, doesn't she?' he'd laugh.

It was quite confusing. The same thing could be taken in completely different ways – treats spoiled me in a bad way if Mum was around, yet they were a way of showing me love if they came from my grandma.

Grandma was a popular lady. When we went out, either on our own or with Mum, she always met lots of people and seemed to have more friends than I could count. Mum didn't have any and hated everyone; her own mother was the exact opposite. When we bumped into one of Grandma's acquaintances, she'd show me off, proudly telling them I was her granddaughter and basking in their compliments. This was all new to me. I wasn't sure what to make of these ladies telling me, and her, that I was gorgeous. I thought I was horrible. I thought I was a nasty child. I couldn't make out whether they were lying or just pretending, because Mum's words carried far more weight in my world than theirs ever could, given that Mum was the one drumming negativity and hatred into me constantly.

Grandma and Granddad always had time for me, and for Mark. Granddad Arthur had been an Army cook in World War Two and he would often tell me stories of his time in the services. He and Grandma would joke that he never seemed to set foot in the kitchen despite his career back then, and it all seemed a very warm and safe environment for me, one which I longed for. The only problem was Mum's jealousy. Even though she was a grown-up, she wanted their attention, especially that of her mother, all the time we were there. I'd often be getting a cuddle from Grandma and catch sight of Mum glaring at me. If Grandma told me she loved me – and she told me that a lot – Mum would wait until we were alone, grab me by the arm, pinch me, and say, 'She loves *me*, not you; she's *my* mother, not yours. She's only saying she loves you to make you feel better; it's me she wants, you're nothing to her.'

This was baffling to say the least. Did it mean that Grandma was lying to me? I couldn't really believe that, because she was so kind to me and it appeared so genuine. I also couldn't bear to let that little bit of happiness go, so I continued to trust Grandma and her words.

'How stupid are you?' Mum would laugh nastily as we walked back to the flat. 'You don't honestly think she cares about you, do you? You don't honestly think she's bothered about a little darkie bastard like you? She tried to kill you, you know. That's how much she loves you. When you were in my belly, she wanted rid of you. She doesn't love you, she loves me. It's me she loves. Not you. You're nothing.'

It would go on and on and on all the way home. By the time we got there, I would be exhausted by the onslaught of her words and any good feelings or happiness I'd had from Grandma would have been washed away by Mum's cruelty.

'Get in there!' she'd shout as soon as she'd opened the door and pushed the pram in. 'Fuck off to your bed – and if you piss in it one more fucking time, you'll be sorry.'

How could I not? How could a five-year-old living in that sort of environment stop wetting herself all of a sudden? It was just one of the ways my body dealt with what was going on, and I could no more prevent it than fly to the moon. I was genuinely trying so hard to make Mum proud and each day that I awoke to wet sheets I would say to myself that it would be the last; I'd work out how to stop doing it. Mum got very cross at me every time it happened, so I would kneel on the floor every night, praying.

'Please, God,' I'd whisper, 'please don't make me wet the bed. If you keep me dry, Mummy will love me and I'll make her happy. Please, God – please help me.'

When I woke up in the morning and the awareness that I was in a damp patch yet again hit me, I'd weep silent tears. Mum would come in, ready to half kill me as usual. She'd drag me out of the bed, often even before checking the sheets, and start shouting at me.

'You fucking wet the bed again! I'm fucking sick of you pissing your own bed, you disgusting little shit!' she'd scream. She'd tell me that she'd had enough and push me against the wall. She would grab hold of the front of my hair and smack me against the wall. You do actually see stars when someone does that to you – I could see little spots swimming in front of my eyes, and they would start to jump about, sparkling like stars but without a shred of beauty. They were there from anger, from hatred, and I couldn't even cry because I knew Mum hated it when I did that.

'Fucking shut up!' she'd screech if I ever cried out in pain.

I would sometimes fear that she was going to kill me. She'd pull out clumps of hair – I actually had bald patches. Sometimes, she'd rip the sheet off the bed. Her strength was terrifying at those times when she was so angry with me, and I'd watch as she wrenched the bedding so hard that the mattress would come off the bed too. Mum would get the wettest part of the sheet and shove it in my face. Her own face would be contorted with hatred as she rubbed and rubbed and rubbed. I'd have friction marks on my face for the rest of the day.

Sometimes she would wash the sheets but she'd never allow me to have a bath, so I smelt. I would never have gone and washed or bathed myself as I couldn't imagine doing things without her say so. If I ever wanted to wash myself, I would have had to ask her and I knew from past experience how it would go.

'Mum,' I'd begin tentatively.

'What?' she'd snap, always ready to assume that I was going to 'bother' her. 'What the fuck do you want now?'

'Can I get washed please?'

'No!' she'd shriek. 'If you fucking smell, you smell. If

someone says you smell and you feel embarrassed, it's your own fucking fault, because you're the one pissing the bed.'

I knew what the reaction would be, so I stopped asking. People did notice. I was at school now, and I would often go into my class knowing, just knowing, that everyone could smell the stench of stale urine coming off me in waves.

There had been no excitement about starting school. Some other little girls might have been counting down the days or going shopping with their mums for a uniform, packing their satchel in anticipation and sharpening their colouring pencils – there was nothing like that for me. One day, Mum just announced I was going to school.

As I got dressed that morning, she said, 'School for you today, thank Christ.'

I was shocked. School had never been mentioned and now it was just thrown at me without warning. I had breakfast and Mum dragged me along the road to where I was going to be taught, one hand on my wrist and one hand pushing my brother in his buggy. It wasn't far, but the whole journey consisted of her warning me to 'Be good . . . don't show me up . . . don't piss yourself . . . behave . . .'

I don't really remember anything about my first day at school, nor much detail of the days that followed. I know that I worried about my smell all the time, and I know that it was hard to make friends because I was already such an isolated, scared little child who had never been taught how to socialize. In fact, most of my memories of school are actually memories of my mum; it's only through writing this book that I've realized just how much she ruled every part of my life. Because I was always so concerned about how she would be with me, and so concerned about how I could turn myself into the daughter she wanted, I didn't think of much else.

Whenever we went to visit Grandma, it was such a relief. At home, I didn't have the life of a five-year-old. I never heard a word of kindness but I also had to do lots of chores that a child twice my age would have struggled with, and I looked after Mark much of the time. To be honest, when I went to Grandma's house, I barely noticed Granddad unless he was telling me his war stories. It was her that I wanted, just like I wanted my mum. The two women were getting closer again, so I hoped that if Grandma loved me some of that might rub off on Mum and she'd love me too. Maybe through Grandma she'd see that I was nice, that although I wasn't Fiona I still deserved her hugs and kisses. Grandma certainly gave me plenty of them, and she was always telling me that I was lovely, and I adored that, even although I knew I'd have to bear Mum's anger on the way home if she overheard any of it. It was a complete novelty to me, and she was the one I hung around when I went for visits, while Granddad was sometimes in the living room or busy with other things.

Grandma treated me in the right way. She recognized that I was five years old, and she never said things to me that were anything other than appropriate. We spoke about dollies and teddies, she bought me pretty dresses and gave me sweets. It was how it should be.

Mum was another matter entirely. At times, I don't

think she even remembered what age I was. She had no friends, and perhaps that was a big part of the problem, for she spoke to me as if I was her best pal rather than her very young daughter.

I remember one day, when I'd been at school for a couple of terms, Mum arrived to pick me up and she was covered in cuts and bruises. This wasn't that unusual, to be honest, but Dad wasn't around at that point, he'd disappeared a few weeks earlier and the endless parade of uncles had started up again.

She said nothing as we walked home with Mark in his buggy, and I was torn between being too scared to ask what was wrong and desperately needing to know. Mum was shaking and quietly crying as we went home, and I'd never seen her so subdued.

'Mummy,' I said, finally plucking up some courage, 'Mummy – what's the matter?'

'Shut up,' she replied. 'Shut up. Nothing's wrong.'

We walked a little more and she kept crying to herself.

'Mummy – please tell me. Maybe I can help?' I begged. 'If you tell me what's happened, maybe I can make it better?' As a child who always wanted things made better, I knew the power of that phrase.

She stopped in the street and put the brake on the buggy.

'You can't. You're just a stupid little girl. How can you make this better?' she said, gesturing towards her ruined face. 'Got a magic wand have you?' She narrowed her eyes at me. 'I've been raped, you stupid little bitch. Tied up, beaten up, knocked out, raped. Sat on like a dog and fucked every which way you can think of. You happy now?

43

You got enough information? Happy to see your mother like this, are you, you little cow?'

With that, she walked on.

Of course, I had no idea what the word meant. Although Mum had no boundaries with me – she would never turn the TV off if there was sex or swearing, she would start kissing the uncles in front of me, and I'd seen violence since the moment I could be aware of it – I'd never heard this word before. I knew it was bad, though. I knew this 'rape' thing was something that had made her look more scared and upset than I had ever seen before. If Dad hadn't done this, and I had no reason to believe he had, this meant that the uncles could turn violent too. Was that just life, I wondered.

The reports did eventually pick up on things, but they had no idea of what I was really being exposed to:

As will be noted from other reports, the pressures under which Sophie lives are most unfavourable. She has been used as an intermediary by her parents. Unfortunately, this has meant that she does not have any friends and has been thrust into the adult world and has missed the pleasures of childhood.

Social work files 4325G/
Sophie Gilmore

So, school didn't really register a great deal with me. I found it all very difficult. I was nervous and didn't settle, I was always thinking about what was waiting for me at home. There were no teachers who noticed the scared child and who rushed in to help her. There was no magic solution to problems. I was invisible.

When I saw my grandma and granddad, it was a relief. We moved to a different house on an even rougher council estate and Mum started going to her parents' house much more often. By the time I was six, we probably saw them every other day. I loved my grandma so much. She idolized me too and that was a complete novelty in my life. It was a natural kind of love, she didn't think about it, she just loved me. I used to sit on her lap and say, 'You're lovely, you are, Grandma,' as I stroked her cheek.

She'd laugh and cuddle me, saying, 'You're lovely too, our Sophie! You're lovely and cuddly and beautiful and I just want to squeeze you and kiss you all day, my darling!'

It was something I'd never had before and I couldn't get enough of it.

Everything about her was perfect in my eyes, even the cigarette smoke she was always surrounded by – it just all seemed comforting. She was glamorous, she always had her hair done and make-up on. She would let me do her nails, no matter what sort of mess I made. Grandma always wore lots of rings, and I was drawn to her engagement ring more than the others.

She'd say to me, 'When I go you can have that ring, Sophie. I promise you.'

'Where are you going, Grandma?' I'd ask, alarmed.

'Oh, I'm going nowhere for a long time, love,' she'd laugh, 'but when I do go to Heaven, I'll smile down on you, knowing that my precious little Sophie is wearing my engagement ring.'

Mum would glare at me when Grandma said that, shooting daggers with her looks. I always knew she was jealous of my relationship with her own mother as she made it perfectly obvious in word and deed.

Grandma loved a bargain, and she was always looking for a good deal at an even better price (I've carried on that tradition too!). She'd take me to these massive jumble sales where she would haggle over even a few pence and pick up all sorts for us as she knew Mum didn't have a lot of money. Grandma loved to buy me clothes and shoes; it didn't matter to me that most of them were second-hand; I just loved that she cared for me enough to give me gifts.

'I love you in fawn,' she always said, bringing something else out of a plastic bag that was the same colour as she always bought me. 'With your eyes and your skin – ooh, you're gorgeous, aren't you, my little darling?'

It was the first time I'd ever heard anything positive about how I looked. I only had a little of my dad's colouring; I wasn't dark-skinned, I just always looked like I had a little bit of a tan, but the fact that Grandma now saw that as a positive thing was very different to Mum screaming, 'You dirty little black bastard!' at me every time I wet the bed.

The big terraced Victorian house in which they lived was a world away from our place. At the front was the kitchen and dining room together. Through the hallway was the living room, but Grandma was always in the kitchen. She was cooking all the time: home-made chips, sausage balls, fish in parsley sauce, cakes and pastries, she was continually making solid food and no one ever went hungry in that house. When she wasn't cooking, she was

46

sewing little things like antimacassars and bits of embroidery. She was just a real home-maker. It was never like that at home, so I wanted to be at Grandma's house whenever I could.

'Sit here,' Granddad would say when I was in his company, patting the sofa next to him. 'Now, be a good girl and keep quiet.' With that, he'd turn his eyes back to Giant Haystacks or whoever was on TV and I'd wait for a few minutes before toddling back through to the kitchen and Grandma. She was the one I wanted to be with; she was the centre of my world really, because at home things were as bad as ever.

One night Mum announced that things were changing.

'I've had enough of you,' she said – one of her stock phrases. 'Come here.'

She dragged me by the wrist into my bedroom and closed the door behind us. Then she locked the door.

'See that?' she asked, pushing her face into mine. 'That's how things are going to be from now on. When you get sent to bed, you're not fucking coming out again.'

The first thing I thought of was the toilet.

'What about if I need the loo, Mum?' I asked.

'Well, I suspect you'll piss the bed as usual, won't you? But if you don't . . .' She unlocked the door and walked off, leaving me standing there, completely confused. A few seconds later, she was back, carrying a plastic bucket.

'There you go,' she said triumphantly, placing it at the side of my bed with a grin on her face. 'Piss in that.'

I was horrified – but there was another thought in my mind.

'What if I need a number two, Mum?' I ventured.

'Are you fucking blind?' she screamed. 'There's a bucket – piss in it, shit in it, do it all in your fucking bed for all I care, just get out of my fucking face! I've had enough of you!'

And with her favourite phrase still ringing in my ears, she was off, locking the door behind her. At weekends, she would sometimes lock me in there too, now that she had the option. I always had to go to my room at six o'clock anyway, whether I was good or not, but there were days when I was in there all the time.

My grandma had bought me a pram for Christmas when I was five, and it was one of the few toys I had. I adored that pram and would spend hours with it, but it also served another important function. If I climbed up on it, I could get on to a window ledge and look out at the other kids who were playing outside. Sometimes, Mum would sneak into the room and all hell would break loose if she saw me doing that. She'd crack me across the head and tell me to get into bed (with plenty of abusive adjectives thrown in for good measure), and I'd lie there, often with sunshine streaming in and the sound of other kids coming through the window into my room, wondering, yet again, why she hated me so very much.

There was barely a day went past that Mum didn't hit me. I couldn't do anything right really but every night before I went to sleep, I hugged myself tightly and thought of what was good in my life. Grandma. I still had Grandma.

Chapter 4

Trying to be a good girl

Sophie presented [herself] as a very confident, self-assured little girl. She [is] a dominant member amongst her peers. Sophie maintains this forthright approach despite its unpopularity with other children. She has found it difficult to relate to the majority of them because of her 'adult' ways – i.e. bossiness, interference and sexual precociousness. Her need to be important and depended upon hinders the making of a reciprocated friendship. With staff, Sophie has reflected the same attitude. She appears self-willed and reluctant to listen to or act upon the advice given her by staff. Recently, she has displayed a more affectionate approach, particularly towards female adults, though easily becomes demanding in this. Sophie has been visited by her mother on several occasions and spent a short weekend at home. Sophie is very guarded about talking in depth about her family. It appears Sophie is heavily depended on by her family. Her behaviour at this time suggests that

she is being given no outlet for her emotional
needs.
Social work files 4325 G/

Sophie Gilmore

I loved it when we went to Grandma's house, and I was even beginning to spend more time with Granddad. He was a big man who always wore heavy woollen cardigans and slippers. I loved Grandma more, but he was nice to me too, even if he did smell a bit. They both smoked like chimneys, but most people did back then so it seemed perfectly normal. Mum wasn't as possessive of him as she was of her mother. She never hissed at me in the same way if Granddad paid me attention, so I supposed that Grandma was her favourite too. My grandparents seemed close to each other. There was none of the fighting that characterized my own parents' relationship, and they only ever gently teased rather than getting into full-blown slanging matches.

Like Dad, my grandfather loved his telly. When he was glued to the screen, I wasn't scared of him in the same way that I was scared of Dad, so I didn't have to crawl across the floor or keep completely quiet, but I was still watching, to see if it was acceptable for me to play like a normal child when he was busy. After a while, I realized it was. He didn't shout at me, and he didn't get angry. Granddad always got me to sit down beside him on the sofa and keep quiet if he was watching something, and now I thought he must like me a bit better too, because he would tell me to sit on his knee when I went through to the living room.

'Come here, young Sophie,' he'd say and I would climb on to his lap. He'd sort of jiggle me about and tickle me, and I enjoyed it. I wished he wouldn't do it quite as much, and I wished that he smelled a bit better when I was close to him, but he wasn't hurting me and he wasn't saying mean things, and I would have gone to anyone who fell into that category. When he had me on his lap, he would put his hands under my armpits and hold me there while he bounced me up and down. It seemed to go on for ages; in fact, it was the only sort of playing he did with me, but I was needy for any sort of attention, so, even although it became boring after a while and it wasn't too comfortable, it was fine by me as there was nothing to be scared of, no words or fists to hide from.

One day, when I was on his lap, he said, 'Let's have you turned round, shall we?'

As he put his hands under my armpits to twist me to face him, my skirt rode up my legs. I always wore skirts, because that was what Grandma bought me; she was quite traditional in that way and never gave me trousers to wear. I tried to pull the skirt down a bit, but Granddad just laughed.

'Don't worry about that,' he said. 'You're just with your old granddad. Nothing to be embarrassed about now, is there?'

And I wasn't. I wasn't embarrassed. I was about six by this time and did feel comfortable around him – why wouldn't I? It was my home life that was hell; my grand-parents' house was a sanctuary. Granddad was always asking me to sit on his lap by that stage, even when he was watching the wrestling or something else on television.

He would tell me that I was lovely, that I was special, and – naturally – I loved it all. He was always saying that I was a real wriggler, that I squirmed about, but I couldn't understand that because I didn't. If he asked me to sit on his lap, I did. If he asked me to turn round, I did. The only time I wriggled or squirmed was if I was facing away from him and he wanted me to turn; then I'd try to pull my skirt or dress down, even although he told me not to bother. I sometimes tried to sit on his lap facing him, trying to guess that he would ask me to do that anyway, but when I did, he would say 'No, no,' and twist me round. Whichever way I sat, I seemed to be facing the wrong direction as he wanted me the other way.

'Stop squirming, you little monkey!' he'd say. 'Who's a naughty girl? It's you, Sophie Gilmore, you're a naughty girl.'

He spoke to me like I was a baby. On one hand, I wanted to tell him that I was really grown-up and that I did lots of grown-up things for my mum, so he didn't need to talk to me like that. I went shopping, I looked after Mum when I needed to, I looked after myself most of the time – and these were all very grown-up things, but, on the other hand, I quite liked being indulged as I never was at home.

It seemed to me that once we started with the wriggling game, Granddad wanted to spend more time with me. Mum and Grandma were often in the kitchen together as Mum tried to keep me away from her when she could so that she would get her mother's undivided attention. So, now that Granddad liked being with me, it suited her down to the ground. On top of that, they went shopping a fair bit and, whereas in the past I'd often gone with them, Granddad was now keen that I stay with him to watch the wrestling. It didn't interest me at all. I would have liked to have seen the kids' programmes, but telly was different back then – there were only a few channels and the programmes for children were only on at certain times, not twenty-four hours a day as they are now. It seemed that wrestling or some other sport was always on though, so that's what we looked at, and that's what Granddad claimed I liked. I didn't say otherwise. When a child is neglected and abused, as I was at home, they take love and attention wherever they can find it. If Granddad was being nice to me – and he was – then I was happy enough to go along with wrestling and the strange jiggling-on-his-knee game. I'd have liked to spend more time with Grandma, of course, but when she came back, she always had something for me.

It seemed that he didn't watch the wrestling all that much anyway while I was on his lap. He would turn me this way and that, twist me backwards and forwards, tickle me and make me giggle. The only thing I didn't like was his smell. It was old and musty and cheesy. I don't know if he ever washed – I didn't very much, but he smelled differently to me. I just tried to not breathe in too much and concentrate on the nice things he was saying to me.

One day, as I sat facing him, all of a sudden, he whipped my skirt up. I was a bit shocked. I knew that it was wrong to show your knickers off as the teachers at school always gave the girls a telling off if they were doing handstands or cartwheels and the boys could see up their skirts. I also knew that it was something grown-ups did, because sometimes the uncles would look up Mum's skirt or I'd catch her showing them her pants.

'Let's have a look at your knickers, then!' he said, as if it was the most natural thing in the world.

I was taken aback. Why would he, my granddad, want to look at *my* knickers? It seemed bizarre. The only thing I could think of that he was checking to see if they were clean. Had Mum told him that I often wet myself? I was relieved that she always made sure I was washed to some extent and had clean underwear on when we went to see my grandparents. She may have only been keeping up appearances, but I would have been horrified if Grand-dad had found that they were smelly. And yet . . . that didn't *seem* to be what he was doing.

He had flipped my skirt up and had a good long look.

I instantly felt uncomfortable, even when I realized my knickers were clean. It was a very odd thing for him to do. I tried to pull my skirt back down again and move, but he held on to me.

'What's your hurry?' he said. 'Stay here.'

He then started bouncing me up and down on his knee. He was holding me on and moving me about quite vigorously. I didn't like it. His knee was pushing into what I knew were my private parts and it was sore. I tried to manoeuvre my body in such a way that there was nothing pressing into me, but whichever way I went, he seemed to put me back to where he wanted me to be. Granddad then started pushing me forward and pulling me back, almost in a rocking motion.

'Do you like that?' he asked. 'Is it fun?'

I didn't like it very much at all, but I did like any sort of attention and I knew from how he was acting and how he was smiling that I was supposed to say how much I was enjoying it too. I also knew that every time he threw me forward he was having a good old look up my skirt. It might have been all right if I had been able to place my body where I wanted, if there had been nothing pushing into me and if I'd had trousers on, but none of those things were the case.

He kept telling me I was a lovely little girl; the compliments came thick and fast – and I revelled in them.

You're a very special little girl, aren't you Sophie?

This is fun, isn't it? You know how to be a good girl.

Granddad loves you very much.

You're very pretty.

This is just the way to spend an afternoon – what a good girl!

And over and over again: 'Let's see your knickers, let's see your knickers, let's see your knickers.'

Eventually, he stopped. Grandma and Mum came in a few minutes after he had got me off his lap and smoothed my skirt down.

'Have a nice time?' he asked them. 'We certainly did – didn't we, Sophie?'

As I smiled and nodded, Mum commented, 'I bet she did. Loves the attention that one. You've made a rod for your own back – she'll be wanting you all the time, the fuss you make of her.'

'That's fine by me,' said Granddad, laughing. 'We always have a lovely time together.'

Again, I just smiled. Mum was right. I did love the attention. I did love the fact that I was warm and fed, that I wasn't being hit, that I was the centre of attention, even if the *type* of attention he gave me wasn't what I wanted at all. From that day on, he made a big fuss of me. He was always wanting to look at my pants, he was obsessed with them. On each visit, he'd manage to get me on my own and he'd lift my skirt up. 'Oh, they're lovely, aren't they?' he'd say. I couldn't see why he was so interested. They were just knickers. Sometimes he'd ask me what type I had on, but before I could answer, he'd say 'No, let me guess!' He would then go through a list, all the while putting his finger to his lips to indicate that I shouldn't say anything.

'Are they pink? Yellow? Are they frilly? I bet they've got lots of lace on them, haven't they? Have they little pictures on? The days of the week? Are they the pretty pale blue ones? Oh, you're a lovely girl for your granddad, aren't you, Sophie?'

The truth was, my knickers weren't special at all. They were cleaner than the ones I wore when I wasn't there, but they seemed to have taken on a huge significance for Granddad. I couldn't understand it, which is natural – how could I possibly have known that this dirty old man was getting sexual kicks from imagining the underwear of a little girl? I assume now that he spent plenty of time when I wasn't there thinking about my knickers, imagining all the various options, so that by the time I did arrive it didn't really matter that I was in some greyish, half-stained misshapen things smelling vaguely of piss; by then he'd already transformed it all in his mind into a paedophiliac fantasy.

Every time I went to their house, he would say, 'Come here, darling, come through to the living room with your granddad.' Mum couldn't wait to get rid of me; she was more than happy to stay in the kitchen with Grandma, chatting and complaining, while I went off with him.

'On my knee then, sweetie,' he'd say as soon as we were on our own, and, from that day on, he always looked up my skirt, always looked at my knickers, always bounced me around and told me that I was having fun. Every time he called me 'darling' or 'sweetie' I cringed – but I also did what he asked. I traded the feeling of discomfort for attention, and it shames me to this day. Paedophiles are so good at finding children who are lost, damaged, alone or different in some way. My grandfather didn't even have to look far; I was right there in his own living room, a child so desperate for attention that I accepted his grooming, seeing it as perfectly normal and natural rather than something I should run from.

Granddad always gave me sweets when I'd been a good girl. He kept a white paper bag of wrapped buttery toffees down the side of the sofa, and whenever we'd 'played' or if it looked as if I was getting ready to climb off, or getting unsettled, he'd reach down the side and pull out a toffee.

'There you go, darling,' he'd say. 'That's for my good girl,' and, while I chewed my sweet, he'd have another look up my skirt, secure in the knowledge that I had my payment.

I knew the shop where he bought the toffee because sometimes Grandma took me there. It had rows and rows of glass jars filled with not just toffee but liquorice, Spanish baccy, cherry lips, Parma Violets, bonbons – all sorts of things. I used to love going there before Granddad began looking at me, but after it had started, I hated even looking at them, knowing what they signified, knowing that they were what I was given when he looked at me in that way I hated. The sweets Grandma gave me tasted nice, especially if they weren't in a white paper bag, but the ones Granddad gave me were starting to taste horrible. They were my hush money. He got to do what he wanted to do; he began to groom me by offering no more than a penny chew.

Granddad did the same things every time; it was like Mum with her OCD, he had a pattern that he followed. He'd tell me to get on his lap, and I'd sit there with a leg on either side. My skirt would be moved up – helped by him – and he'd suggest we play a game. The game was always him bouncing me about as he moved my skirt still higher and his hands went up my legs. Every time I tried to shuffle away, he'd pull me back and do the quiet joking about me being a 'squirmer'. If there was ever a sudden noise, or it sounded like Grandma was coming through, he'd shove me off his knee as quick as a flash and yet, despite this, he would also constantly tell me that it was all fine, I wasn't to worry, we were having a lovely time. He spoke as if this was a happy thing to do and I did wonder whether I was getting it wrong. He was so nice to me usually; it was just this one thing that made me feel uncomfortable, so, as always I questioned myself and my habit for getting things wrong and messing them up, just as Mum always told me I did.

'There's nothing to worry about,' he'd whisper.

But I was worried.

I was worried that he would stop liking me if I didn't start enjoying the game, so I tried, I really did. I tried to not breathe in when I was on his lap, so that the cheesy stench that came from him didn't get into my nostrils. I tried to not feel his knee digging into my private parts. I tried to not notice the big, hard thing that poked up from the front of his trousers. In fact, that was the thing I tried to avoid more than anything. I had a sense that if I spoke about it or drew attention to it, things would get worse. When Mum had her boyfriends round, she never bothered to hide anything. It didn't matter to her whether I was in the room when they started kissing and touching each other, and I had often been there, watching, while she touched them *there* or when they guided her hand down the front of their trousers. When that happened, they seemed to laugh or they would make strange grunting noises that also seemed to make them happy, but I wanted nothing to do with that. I would do the game, I would pretend to enjoy, but I did have a foreboding that it should go no further, that I should ask no questions and draw no attention to the hard stick thing in Granddad's trousers. I hated it when he pushed it against me while we 'played' and I knew that it was something that should be hidden, because when he shoved me off his lap and Grandma entered the room, he would place a cushion over it for a while. If she wasn't meant to see it, then I certainly wanted to keep away from it, I knew that for certain.

It felt horrible that the one place I had felt safe was now tainted. Home was as bad as ever. I was at school, but didn't go that often. If Dad was back and hitting Mum, there were plenty of days when she wouldn't get out of bed to take me there (Dad never did); I can only assume there were times that she couldn't bear people seeing the damage he had inflicted on her, or perhaps she was even in too much pain to get up. Looking back, I feel heartily sorry for what my mum went through with him. She was vile to me, she made my life a living hell and I hate her for that, but I also know that she was going through hell too – I just can't see why she would take it out on a little girl. I was now six, but she had been awful to me since Fiona's death; did it make her feel better in some way to pick on a child? Or had something snapped in her with the loss of that baby and she didn't actually know what she was doing? She was cleaning constantly and muttering things under her breath, but I have no idea how far her mental health problems went, or even whether they would be categorized as that because she did keep herself and Mark clean, and she did look after him and manage to deal with people on her terms. She never had a breakdown as such, she never acted inappropriately in front of others – she was just the mother from hell to me.

Whatever the reason for her behaviour, it was a never-ending nightmare. Even when Dad wasn't around, school seemed like an optional extra. There were days when Mum couldn't be bothered to take me, days when she wouldn't unlock my bedroom door until after lunchtime. Days when she was too busy with the 'uncles' to realize she had a child to look after or too busy cleaning to notice anything, leaving me to look after Mark while she dusted and vacuumed and moved things. Sometimes I would hear Grandma come to take Mark for the day so he escaped. Grandma must have assumed on those occasions that I was at school, and I knew better than to make any noise from my room to let her know otherwise, and then I'd hear her go off with my little brother, while I languished in my own filth for the rest of the day.

One day, a man came to our front door late at night – well, it seemed late at night to me, but that could have meant that it was winter and it was dark early. I was in the living room with Mum and Mark, but I was close to the door. I heard the bell and she whispered to me to stay still, not to go any closer.

She held Mark close to her and put a finger to her lips to indicate I should keep quiet. After a little while, I heard the letterbox opening.

'Is there anyone there?' the man shouted.

After a few moments, he continued, 'I know there is – I know you're in there, Jennifer.'

Mum said nothing. It didn't sound like one of the 'uncles'. The man seemed quite calm and well-spoken. I had no idea who he was. I heard him say, 'Jennifer? You know why we're here, don't you?'

She glowered at me, making it clear that I was to remain silent.

'Jennifer!' he went on. 'It's about Sophie – you know that.'

I was shocked to hear my own name. How did this man know who I was – and what did he want with me? I reached out to hold Mum's hand, but she snatched it away from me.

'Jennifer – please open the door,' he said in a low voice. 'You know that I need to take Sophie with me. We've spoken about this; she needs to be taken into care and it's time.'

I had no idea what was going on. I didn't know what

'taken into care' meant. Mum thrust Mark into my arms and launched herself at the door. It was still closed and locked, but she began screaming at the man on the other side.

'Fuck off! Just fuck off! You're not getting in! You're not getting anything, so just fuck off!'

I could hear him talking quietly, trying to calm her down from the other side, but I couldn't hear exactly what he was saying as she was making so much noise. All I knew was that she was swearing and screeching. I held Mark in my arms and tried to distract him while it all went on. Eventually, the noise stopped and Mum came back into the living room.

'Is he all right?' she asked, taking my little brother from my arms and kissing him tenderly. I nodded. 'Get to your room,' she snapped at me. I started to talk, needing to know what was going on. All I got in reply was a slap across the head and a command, again, to go to my room.

Of course, I had – and still have – little idea of what had brought about the visit from the man who said I needed to be taken into care. I knew that the neighbours were always complaining about us, because I was often there when they came to the door, saying that there was too much noise, saying that they couldn't get any peace. Mum – or Dad if he was there – would just launch a stream of obscenities at them and it would all settle down until the next time. I didn't know whether someone had complained about me being in the middle of all that, or whether a teacher at school had said something about my many absences. How would I know? Mum barely spoke a civil word to me at the best of times, never mind took me into her confidence unless it was to talk to me about her sex life. Her response to the man at the door had been, I think, a desire to keep Mark, not me. I'm sure she would have been happy to see the back of me, but he was her golden boy and perhaps she thought that, if she let one child go, it would be easier for the authorities to take the one she truly cared about.

My files do show that things were being looked into, but they also show that, despite Mum and Dad admitting to taking things out on me, nothing was done. The only thing that happened was that a vague promise was extracted for Mum and Dad to accept help.

Mrs Gilmore described her behaviour towards Sophie as, on occasion, taking things out on her. It became apparent that when the marriage was going through a bad patch, Sophie became the focus for the parents' discontent and frustration. I raised the issue with the parents and both admitted that punishment of Sophie had little to do with her behaviour but rather had to do with them themselves and the way they were feeling. Mrs Gilmore was insistent that under no circumstances would she give Sophie up. I asked her why she wanted to keep her and she said Sophie was her daughter and she would care for her. Following discussions . . . it was decided that no immediate Place of Safety need be taken but that Sophie be allowed to remain at home provided that the parents agreed to a social worker becoming involved with them.

Social work files 4325G/

Sophie Gilmore

63

Looking at those files, I feel that was a missed opportunity. There was so much the authorities didn't know but surely even the little they *did* know was enough for them to do something?

Nothing else was said about it, but a few weeks later, when I came back from one of my rare days at school, there was another man waiting at our door. He was tall with thick, thick eyebrows that I still remember. He was carrying a briefcase, and I just knew that he was 'official', not one of Mum's boyfriends.

'Hello,' he said, as soon as we got to the door. 'You must be Sophie.' He got on his knees so that he was at my height when he spoke to me, and gave me a big smile.

'Fuck off,' said Mum, who rarely said anything else to outsiders.

'This won't do, Jennifer,' he told her in a very serious voice. 'You must know that yourself.'

'Didn't you hear me?' she replied. 'Fuck off. Now.'

The man did leave, but when I got to school the next day, he was in my classroom. Mum hadn't seen him as she always dropped me off at the gate and left straight away, before the bell even rang if I was early enough. The man with the big bushy eyebrows was talking to my teacher and to the head teacher, who I didn't really know at all. I sat down at my desk and the man smiled at me kindly just as he had the day before.

My teacher – Miss Marsden – came over to me. She was a big woman with bright red hair and lots of lipstick.

'Sophie,' she said. 'This gentleman wants to have a word with you.'

In my head, I knew what I was meant to say, Mum had

told me plenty of times. Nothing was anyone's business outside the family and I should have told him to 'fuck off' just as she would have done, but he seemed a nice man and I didn't want to be rude, I wanted to be a good little girl, so I went with him to one of the school offices. Everyone was looking at me as he took me away and what I remember was – I liked that, I liked that bit of attention.

He asked me so many questions, and I can't truly remember all of them, but there was a lot about my mum and dad, whether anyone was hitting me, whether I was happy. I answered all the questions as if Mum was sitting there, listening. Even back then, Mum had drilled it into me that I wasn't to dare tell anyone what my life was like.

'If you do . . .' she used to say, but she'd never finish the sentence. Her face would screw up until it was really ugly, despite the fact that she was a very attractive lady usually, and she'd look so threatening that I knew I'd never tell a soul. When I was in that room with the bushy-eyebrowed man, I remembered every warning she'd ever given me.

'Are you happy at home, Sophie?'
Yes.
'Is your mum nice to you?'
Yes.
'Is your dad nice to you?'
Yes.
'Does anyone hit you?'
No.
'Are you fed regularly?'
Yes.
'Does anyone say bad things to you?'
No.

'Are you worried about anything?'

No.

'Is there anything you'd like to tell me, Sophie?'

YES, YES, YES my head screamed, but *no, no, no* was what came out of my mouth.

The man looked at me as if he knew. There was something in his eyes that told me that he had a complete understanding of what was happening, but if I didn't say anything he couldn't help. I have thousands of pages of files from my childhood but I can find no record of that meeting. I wonder why.

It was an additional opportunity for me, but it slipped away and I was taken back to my classroom where everyone stared at me again. Mum had drummed it into me so hard that it was us against the world that I hadn't said a word. No matter how horrible she was to me, and no matter how uncomfortable I was at what Granddad was doing, I just knew that I wasn't supposed to speak up. Inside, I wondered whether this would be enough to make her like me. Maybe when I got home that day she would somehow know what had happened and she'd do what I'd always dreamed of. She'd take me in her arms and say, 'Oh Sophie! You're a lovely little girl! I love you so much, I really do.'

I'd been good. I'd lied to the man, but I'd lied because I was protecting my mummy. That made me a good girl – didn't it?

The following day there was a man at our door yet again – a new one, but this time carrying a briefcase and lots of papers. This time it was a different Jennifer Gilmore who spoke to him and I was astounded when

Mum let him into the house. Perhaps she'd known he was coming and had decided this was the best way to avoid trouble. The place was spotless, although it always was, and I remember the man saying how clean it was, as if he was very impressed.

Mrs Gilmore appears to be in her mid-twenties, attractive and well-dressed. The home was clean and tidy and showed good standards of housekeeping. The children seemed clean and healthy and there was no sign of injury on them.
Social work files 4325G/
Sophie Gilmore

And that was it. The social worker had seen all he wanted to that time. Mum was attractive, the kids were clean, the house was spotless – what more could they possibly hope for? I was invisible again and Mum was doing a perfect job of pretending.

Still, I wanted someone to help me and still no one did.

Chapter 5

Happy families

Sophie has shocked many children with her
reference to sexual matters. She has deliberately
urinated in the wastepaper bin. She has encoun-
tered many problems with other children due to
her precocious manner.
Social work files 4325G/
Sophie Gilmore

Mum had another baby when I was six, another little boy.
This time the baby was called Alex. I watched and waited
to see how she would be with him, not knowing what I
wanted. If she was horrible to him, like she was to me,
I would feel bad because he was only a tiny baby, but it
would show that it wasn't just me she hated. If she was
nice, and loved him like she loved Mark, I would know
that it was all my fault.

She loved him – which meant that it was all down to
me. She could be a good mummy, I could see that, but she
needed the right type of child for that to happen, and I
was clearly wrong. Dad was still in and out of our lives –

obviously long enough at times for Mum to get pregnant, but he was never a stable presence or a good role model. All my files and reports allude to the same features and characteristics in me time after time – I was sexually aware, I was manipulative in the sense that I could make people think things were fine when they were far from that, I was old beyond my years, I'd been given too much responsibility. They were right with all of that; it was what I was living day after day.

My problems continued. I was still wetting the bed a lot, but I had also found a way to soothe myself. I had started to rock myself – especially to sleep – to get comfort, and also to shake my leg up and down, as I found the constant movement relaxing. I was always nervous, and when I was in my room alone, I cried my heart out. I sobbed so much that I could barely catch my breath, and that's how I would spend my time, alone and heartbroken. When I was that age there was nothing in my life that offered hope apart from my grandma, but that was now tempered by the way in which Granddad was treating me. In front of others, I could be different – just like Mum. The terrified little girl I really was would disappear and there were times when I would become bolshy, confident and willing to take on anyone, even though I was feeling a long way from that inside. That's so often the way with neglected or abused children – they are being raised in a way that shows there is one face for the outside world and one for private, so they develop the same. Some of them – like me – get into trouble. They seem like tearaways, but, all the time, their hearts are breaking and they just desperately want someone to recognize what is really going on in their lives and take them away from the horror.

Mum despised me and was also teaching Mark to hate me as well. He would say things to taunt me, and say how horrible I was. I had loved him so much that it cut me to the bone when he began to chant in a singsong voice, 'Sophie's stupid! Sophie smells!' I still loved him, but I hated the idea that the little boy I loved was turning against me, and I suspected the same would happen with Alex when he was old enough. I tried to protect them when I could. Mum sometimes hit them, not to the extent she battered me and she was always apologetic afterwards with her boys, but I would do what I could to stand between them if possible to take extra blows – to take the blame for everything if it meant my little brothers could be spared some of the agony. She was free with her hands, but her spiteful tongue was only ever let loose on me. I was hit more and hit harder than the boys without a doubt, but I was also privy to her sexualized stories and to her verbal abuse. That was our special mummy-daughter time and no one else was involved. She saved all that for me.

There was no escape really. I had no friends, no houses I could go to after school, no playmates to distract me from what was going on at home and at Grandma's house. There was still a lot of racism directed at me and my skin colour made some children wary and made others see me as someone to be taunted and insulted. Like my mother they would call me anything that seemed like a racist slur, they didn't care how accurate it was. On top of that, I didn't know how to be around other children. I never had friends round my house, I never went to play parks or ballet classes, and I was always being told by Mum to trust no one. I found school very difficult as nothing seemed to stick in my brain, probably because I had never been raised in a way that would make learning fun or enjoyable. Mum had never taught me the alphabet, and she had never sat with me drawing pictures or colouring in. The only thing she had started to do was her version of counting. It wasn't a matter of teaching me one, two, three; instead, she had a way of asking questions that were very specific.

'If I bought a pint of milk at eleven pence and handed over a pound, how much change would I get?' she'd ask. 'If I bought a loaf as well for thirty-eight pence, how much change would I get?' My head would swim, but if I got it wrong I would see stars as well as she would hit me instantly. 'For Christ's sake, Sophie!' she'd shout. 'You need to know these things! I can't do everything for you; it's time you pulled your weight.' With that, off she'd go again, quizzing me on prices and counting money until I could have wept. I was always trying so desperately to learn, but I couldn't do it and being disliked at school made it worse. I never really had friends to fall back on and I wasn't clever; I was just as useless as Mum said.

When Alex was born, Dad came back for longer than usual. I don't know why, I don't know whether having three children made him feel that he should try to be a family man for a while, but it didn't work. He was hitting Mum less, I do remember that, but they were constantly screaming and shouting at each other.

'He's a bastard,' Mum would tell me. 'Never forget that — if anyone does ask you and you squeal, just remember; it's all his fault, everything's his fucking fault, the dirty Paki bastard.'

I started to believe her, and maybe she was right – how would I know? I didn't know how she'd been before him, neither of us knew how she would have been if she'd ended up with a good man instead of him. The years of violence, the constant threat of violence even when it didn't happen, must do something to a woman. There was very little public discussion of domestic abuse back then and it was all largely hidden. How do I know how she would have been if she'd got out early on? How do I know what sort of mum she would have been if Dad hadn't knocked her senseless every time he was there? There is no excuse for the behaviour of either of them, but perhaps Mum was more of a victim than I sometimes give her credit for. I still don't know how she could have beaten and tormented and tortured a small child the way she did, but I did start to absorb her message that everything was Dad's fault. She would tell me it over and over as she hit me too.

You're your father's fucking daughter all right!

This made me think she was only hitting me because I reminded her of the man she hated.

You're the dead spit of that filthy bastard!

This made me think that if I looked more like her and less like him, she'd love me more.

I could have had a fucking life if I hadn't been shackled to him because of you, you little bastard.

This made me think that she wished she had aborted me back when Grandma had wanted to put her in a boiling bath.

It all came back to the same thing – I was six years old and would have done anything to get the love I craved.

The whole family was falling apart, but from the files I have, I can see that, despite the many reports being written, little action was taken. The visits by the men who had said they were going to take me away and who asked whether I was ill-treated seemed to have fizzled away to nothing. Never a day passed without some neighbour or other at our door, complaining about the noise, but they were always sent away with a barrage of abuse. They gave up after a while and only got the police involved when things were so loud that they really couldn't be ignored.

Mum was just as loving with Alex as she was with Mark, whereas Dad was pretty much the same with all of us; he couldn't be that bothered one way or another. When he was there Mum didn't lock me in my bedroom and she didn't put the bucket in there for me to use as a toilet, so it was better in that sense. She also waited until his back was turned or he was distracted before she would unleash her usual hatred on me. She still pulled my hair and hit me, but not in front of him. I don't know why she bothered hiding it, because he was knocking hell out of me too. I was the punch bag for both of them, and whenever anything went wrong between them, they picked on me and I was caught in the crossfire.

Although I was desperate for Mum's love, I wasn't that bothered about Dad. I really didn't care whether he was around or not. He paid me little attention, so I did feel that it was out of character one night when he came in while I was in bed trying to get to sleep. I assumed I was in for another beating for something I couldn't even remember doing (not that there ever needed to be something specific).

I had an old-fashioned bed with a sprung mattress and a brown headboard. There was a light attached to the headboard and it was still switched on as I was quite scared of the dark. Dad came over and pulled the cord so that the room was in darkness, apart from a little slither of light coming in from the streetlamps. I had no idea why he was there; I wasn't a child who got night-time stories or lullabies, and the only experience I had of a parent coming in to see me was when Mum was shouting or hitting me or sniffing my sheets.

Dad shook me a little by the shoulders – he must have thought I was already asleep as my eyes had been closed when he came in, but that was because I always felt it was better to pretend to be asleep when Mum came to see me, just in case she could be fooled and I could escape her wrath.

'Sophie,' he said, quietly. 'Sophie!'

I didn't answer him, but peeked without opening my eyes fully. He was in his red nylon pyjamas, ready for bed too. I wondered whether he was coming in to say 'night night'. It was unlikely; no one had ever bothered before. He reached under the covers and took my hand, drawing it out towards him as he sat on the bed close to me.

'Sophie – wake up!' he commanded, and I opened my eyes fully. I felt embarrassed – Dad's pyjama trousers had fallen open when he sat down and I could see everything as he sat there. The pyjama bottoms had a hole in the front (I didn't realize that men had these sorts of holes in their pyjamas and pants so that they could wee, I just

74

thought he'd ripped them and didn't know) and, somehow, all his private parts were on display. I couldn't say anything in case he became as embarrassed as I was, so I kept quiet and didn't look.

But – something odd was happening.

Dad was guiding my hand towards what was sticking out of his pyjama trousers.

'Touch it,' he was whispering to me, and I was very confused. Why would I touch *that*? It was private, it was nothing to do with me and it looked horrible. I knew that Mum touched those *things* on her boyfriends, and I knew that the hard stick thing Granddad had in his trousers was related to this in some way, but I didn't think these *things* had anything to do with me and I wanted to keep it that way.

'Touch it, touch it,' he kept saying.

He was quite out of breath and seemed excited. I was shaking my head and saying no but all he could repeat was 'touch it, touch it,' over and over again. It didn't matter how many times he said it, I would *never* want to touch *that*.

I have thought about this so many times and I genuinely can't think of anything that led up to that horrible moment. Dad had never said anything, or done anything, that would suggest that he was building up to getting me to touch him or grooming me in any way. That, after all, was Granddad's department. What he did went from nothing – from him not even having been there most of the time – to *that*. I had never seen him look at me strangely. He had never said strange things to me like Granddad did. He had never asked to see my knickers or guessed what colour I was wearing. He had never given me sweets from a paper bag while he told me I was his special girl. So, why this?

I didn't want to do it. I really didn't want to do it. He pushed my hand on to his private area and started pushing it about. I could smell him; he always had a sweaty scent about him, and it seemed stronger at that moment. He didn't smell horrible like Granddad, he didn't have the cheesy smell, but I still pulled away from him. He smelled like my dad, he always smelled that way, but he wasn't acting like a dad.

It, the thing, looked black in the weak light coming from the streetlamp. It scared me. It looked huge and frightening, and I had never seen anything like it. The horrible fact was, however, that I had heard of these things, and I knew it was a penis. Mum used to say really inappropriate things to me. She often didn't treat me like I was her daughter, never mind one that was only six years old. When she wasn't beating seven shades of shit out of me, or mentally tormenting me, she was talking to me as if I was her sister or friend, so if she'd had a boyfriend round she'd chat about him when he left.

'Oh, he so wanted me,' she'd say.

'When I touched him, he got huge – absolutely huge.'

'He was desperate for me. Couldn't wait to have me.'

'My God – he was massive; I can hardly walk – you should have seen the things he did to me!'

These were all comments I had to listen to regularly. She'd talk about what had happened, and what they had done, as soon as the men left. It was almost as if she didn't realize who she was talking to; she just needed someone, and seemed completely oblivious to how wrong it was for a mum to chat to her own child in that way. Half of the time, I had no idea what she was talking about – she spoke about sex to me, but it was often in a nudge-nudge sort of way: filthy, inappropriate talk that assumed I knew what she meant, though I didn't a lot of the time. Sex was always there but I'd never had a biology lesson; I didn't actually know a lot of things. What did she mean when she said he got huge? The man had looked the same to me when he left. What did she mean when she said he couldn't wait to have her? These things were a mystery to me, but I knew that I was just meant to listen, not question. She saw me as an outlet, I think. Maybe it was because she was young – she was only about twenty-two at this point of my life – and possibly had no idea about what the boundaries should be. Sometimes when I think about Mum, I do try to give her the benefit of the doubt – but then I wonder what sort of person would *ever* think it was all right to discuss their sex life with a child. She had also told me that she didn't like having sex with my dad – he was 'crap' apparently. Even though I didn't really understand a lot of what she was saying, I was absorbing it.

When Dad forced me to touch him, I knew it was related to all those things Mum had been talking about. He was pulling my hand backwards and forwards as I shook my head and told him 'no' over and over again. It didn't matter. He ignored me, and I hated it.

I didn't know what he wanted me to do, what the *purpose* of it was. Looking back, I know that he didn't ejaculate, but, at that point, I didn't know that was what he was trying to do. After a while, just as his breathing got more laboured, he quickly got up off the bed and left my room. I was left lying there crying and wondering what I had done to deserve that. I didn't sleep that night. I feared that he would come back and do something else, even if I wasn't sure what the something else would be. By the time morning came, I was exhausted. I hadn't slept so hadn't wet the bed and it was ironic that I escaped Mum's anger just because I had been too petrified to do what came naturally.

Dad wasn't there when I got up and when he did come back at dinner time he ignored me, which was pretty usual. I tried to convince myself that I had either imagined it or that he had been sleepwalking. It was a mistake, and it wouldn't happen again – I crossed my fingers and prayed that was the case.

It wasn't.

The following night, and the night after that, and the night after that, Dad was back again. It always followed the same pattern. Everyone liked patterns in my life. He'd turn the light off, tell me to wake up, take my hand and rub it up and down on his penis. He would get excited, hot and bothered, then leave the room quickly, while I lay there confused and ashamed. It never occurred to me to tell Mum – why would I? Somehow I knew that, if I did, it would result in me being hit more and that she would probably never believe me in the first place anyway.

After about a week of this, Dad seemed to be getting more and more frustrated, and there was a new development. When he had been moving my hand up and down on him for a while he lifted up my nightdress with his other hand and looked at me. I had no knickers on – they were all in the wash or waiting to be washed if they had been soiled when I wet the bed – and I was so ashamed that he was able to stare at my private parts. Granddad had already looked up my dress, but I always had my pants on. In fact, Granddad would always actually say, 'Go on – let me have a look at your knickers.' While I hated that, it was even worse to know that I had no knickers on at all – no covering, nothing to hide me.

Dad just stared and stared and stared. He then started moving my hand over his private parts even faster than before, grunting a lot, then he cast my hand aside and began touching himself all the while looking at me. When I tried to pull my nightdress back down, he would grunt 'No!' angrily, and I would know better than to go against him. Humiliated and mortified, I lay there, letting him violate me with his eyes, before finally, as usual, he left the room in a hurry as I wept silent tears.

When I think of those times, I remember his breathing very clearly. In fact, as I write this, I can hear it. It haunts me. There was always so much of it – such panting, such intense laboured gasps – and then he would go off to the bathroom. I'd hear him lock the door; Mum was asleep, my brothers were asleep – or, at least, I assumed they were – so I was having to deal with this on my own. Did Mum know? I have no idea. I'd put nothing past her, but I did know that if I said anything she'd find a way to blame me. So, I kept quiet. I kept quiet about Dad, just as I kept quiet about Granddad, and just as I'd kept quiet about Mum. I was good at keeping quiet – but I hoped that someone would still know how to hear me.

At school something odd had happened; I'd made a friend. Katy was a bit like me, she stood away from everyone else at playtime and lunch, and she got called names too. She was very overweight and so was obviously called 'fatty' by everyone. I didn't join in the name calling and, after a while, we just gravitated towards each other. We didn't say that much but it was as if we had a sense that we were kindred spirits. The odd, left-out children often don't need to speak to know they'll get on. No one else wants them anyway. They're picked last for team games. They're avoided when other kids choose who to sit next to. They never get prizes or awards. They smell or are fat or are skinny or are weird in a thousand other ways that mark them out – and that was what drew me to Katy and Katy to me. I wouldn't say that she changed my school life, but it was certainly a little more bearable to know that there was someone I could stand or sit next to at playtime and lunch, even if we didn't say much.

After a while, I decided to take a huge step and ask Mum if Katy could come round to play one day. I knew it was what 'normal' kids did, and thought I should at least go through the motions.

She surprised me by answering, 'Maybe,' but then wasn't able to resist having a dig about how there might be hope of me not being such a weirdo after all.

'Got a friend at last, have you?' she taunted. 'I suppose she's as queer as you – never mind, bring her round and I can have a laugh!'

It seemed so unlikely that Mum would really agree that I didn't follow it up straight away. I assumed that she would get my hopes up, and then, on the day, deny she had agreed to anything. However, Katy kept asking when she could come over and, eventually, I became worried that I might lose my new friend if I didn't pluck up the courage to raise the subject with Mum again.

When I did, I was surprised once more.

'Have her round for a sleepover if you like,' Mum said to me. 'Treat yourself – pretend you're normal.' She found this comment hilarious, and went off laughing.

When I told Katy the next day, she was beside herself with excitement. It opened things up between us and we chatted non-stop. What I remember is the planning – what we would do, what we would talk about, how late we would stay up. What I didn't tell Katy was that it was very, very unlikely that it would ever happen.

However, amazingly, it did. Mum didn't tell me it was all in my imagination, she actually kept to her word. When I took Katy home that day after school, I was the happiest I could ever remember. I had spent the whole day with knots in my tummy, thinking that something would happen soon to prevent it. I thought Mum would turn up at the school gate to say 'no', I thought she would turn Katy away when we got to the house – I imagined every way it could end up not happening, but it did, it happened.

We played as well as we could with the few toys I had and when we finally went to sleep, we planned to giggle and chat all night. It didn't work out that way, of course, and we fell asleep within minutes, exhausted with the thrill of it.

I don't know how long I had been asleep when I felt the familiar sensation of Dad pulling on the sleeve of my nightdress. I couldn't believe that, tonight of all nights, with Katy there, he wanted to touch me and show me his disgusting thing.

'Sophie, Sophie,' he whispered. 'Sophie, wake up.'

'No, Dad,' I hissed as loudly as I dared, terrified in case Katy woke up. 'Katy's here, go away!'

I was sure that would send him off; he must have just forgotten that I had a friend round because it had never happened before.

Again, I told him, 'Remember – Katy's here, go away!'

'I know she is, I know,' he smiled.

Then, to my horror, he did what he always did and put my hand on his thing, using his own to make me rub it and push it up and down as his breathing got more and more laboured. I was desperate for him to leave, so I just hoped that he would be quick and get out. He lifted my nightdress up to have a look and I prayed it would all be over soon. Appallingly, to my mind, he seemed to be making even more noise than usual and was in no hurry. To my shock, Katy woke up.

Her eyes nearly popped out of her head when she saw what was going on and she screamed.

'Hello, Katy,' said Dad. 'Do you want to touch it?'

I couldn't believe what I was hearing. This should never have happened, but I knew it was wrong for him to do anything but go away. If he'd done that, maybe I could have persuaded Katy in the morning that it had been a dream – now what would I do?

She began crying and shook her head, backing away into the corner of the bed as far away from him as she could possibly get.

'Get her to do it,' said Dad. 'Get her to touch it, Sophie.'

'No!' I shouted. 'No, Dad, it's wrong.'

'It is not,' he laughed. 'It's fine, just get her to touch it like you do.'

He had a horrible look on his face, evil and twisted, as he surely was at that moment.

To my eternal shame, I thought the only way to get rid of him was to do as he said. If he was right, if this was all fine and other daddies and granddads did it with other little girls, perhaps all that was worrying Katy was the colour of Dad's thing.

'It'll be all right, Katy,' I said, 'he just wants you to touch it a little bit. Don't be scared – it's like a normal one, just a different colour.'

The poor girl looked terrified, as she should have been. She started screaming and I heard my mum yell, 'Shut the fuck up and get to sleep.'

It all went silent for a while, ominously quiet. Then I heard her say, 'Ali? Where the fuck are you?'

Dad winked at us and left the room.

I had a father who wanted to abuse me and my only friend. I had a mother who saw nothing wrong with him disappearing from her bed in the middle of the night while a little girl screamed in terror.

And I lost my only friend.

Katy didn't sleep that night and, in the morning, she sat at the door waiting for her Mum for hours. She never spoke to me again, and I can't blame her. I wish I could go back in time and change that night; I wish I had never tried to make her do those terrible things and I'm only grateful that she was stronger than me.

I'm sorry, Katy – I'm so sorry.

For me, it went on for a while. Dad got me to touch him pretty much every night when he was there for that 'visit', which is how I thought of his time with us. He went away after a month or so in the wake of another huge fight with Mum, and by the time he came back, both of the boys were of an age where he could play with us all together. He had never really been the sort of father who did play much, but there was something different about him when he returned. He would get us all in the living room and play in a very physical way. There was a lot of contact, a lot of tickling, a lot of touching. It reminded me of how Granddad played and I hated it.

I remember at one point he was holding me down on the floor with one hand, play-fighting, and he'd chased my brothers out of the room. They were full of giggles – Alex could barely walk, he wasn't even a year old, but he could toddle, and he was hooting with laughter. As soon as they had gone, Dad put his hand up my skirt and into my knickers. He smiled and said 'Quiet, just keep quiet,' as if we were sharing a lovely secret rather than being in the middle of an abusive nightmare. He smiled at me and touched me in places he shouldn't have as I listened for my brothers and prayed that they would save me as I had saved them so many times in the past.

The boys ran in again. Dad had to do no more than roar at them like a pretend lion for them to run off and he touched me again. He was moving his fingers and hand all over me, inside my knickers, over my private parts and it was horrible. He was doing the heavy breathing and panting that he did at bedtime. After a few more moments, Alex and Mark returned, wanting to be chased.

'Up on my back, Sophie,' Dad said. I couldn't remember him ever giving me a piggyback before, but I clambered on, relieved to be escaping his horrible hands moving all over me. Little did I know that, once on his back, even although we were chasing my little brothers around the room, he had one hand holding on to me and another inside my knickers again. He was touching me all the time. I desperately wanted to get off, but he was too strong, holding on and also telling me to sit still.

Every time that we played after that he would tell me to get on his back and I knew he would touch me privately. A few weeks later, Dad disappeared once more, and when he came back the abuse stopped just as suddenly as it had started. He never touched me on any other occasion, but while he had been there it had gone on for months.

That was my experience of happy families – and it seemed to be getting worse by the day. I've often wondered – if I had been asked the right questions, would I have told anyone what was going on?

Yes.

Yes.

Yes.

If I had been made safe and if I had been told that it was all going to be fine, I would have sung my heart out. But no one did that. I was just Sophie the troublemaker, and my troubles were mine to shoulder alone.

Chapter 6

Time to grow up

Sophie is familiar and self-confident in liaising with
agencies and has perhaps missed out on the
little-girl stage of her development and conse-
quently finds it difficult to play with her peer
group. Sophie is still enuretic.
Social work files 4325G/
Sophie Gilmore

I was being touched by my dad and by my granddad at this
point. Mum was telling me all about what went on between
her and her boyfriends. I felt as if it was everywhere.
Everything was sex, sex, sex. I know now, of course, that
this makes it even less likely that a child will tell, because
they think that abuse is the norm, they think it's everywhere. I only had two male figures in my life really – and
they were both abusing me. All the other men, the ones
who hung around Mum, were fleeting, so I was left with
the ones who should have cared for me, who should have
protected me instead of violating me and making me feel
that this was just what happened to all little girls.

I wondered whether there was something wrong with me. If this was going on in other families and they didn't say anything, there *must* be something wrong with me because I absolutely hated it. Yet again, it was my fault; I felt that it was something wrong with me, not my dad and my granddad.

We were a notorious family. In most deprived areas – and in some that aren't so deprived – I think there's always a family that everyone knows. A family that causes more trouble than everyone else, a family that seems to attract trouble as well as dish it out. That was us. That was the Gilmores. Our name was synonymous with everything bad. Even when we weren't responsible for something that had happened, we got the blame because we had been behind so much disruption in the past. Not only were we known to everyone in Social Services and beyond, but the neighbours had us marked out too.

We made more noise than anyone else because there always seemed to be a fight going on in our house, and I was usually the one on the receiving end of someone's fist. If there wasn't a fight, there would be noise of some other description. On top of that, due to Mum's OCD, she would clean at all hours of the day and night. The police were often at our door – when I got my files, however, there was no record of those reports, so I can only assume that there is an even bigger pile of records on us somewhere else. One of the things that was striking from the files I did receive, though, was just how many missed meetings there were. There were no mobile phones or email back then, so the social-work department, housing, child abuse or welfare people always wrote to Mum to let her know when they were coming. Those letters are there, and so are many that log that she wasn't there when they turned up. More would be set up – and she would defiantly miss many of those too. When they did get her, she would apologize, act contrite and the whole pattern would start all over, making it clear to me reading the files that she was only letting people see her, us and the house when it suited her, on her terms.

This seems very wrong to me. Whenever I read a story or hear something on the news about a neglected or abused child who has died despite official involvement, a chill runs down my spine. I'm furious that children are still being ignored and unseen, unhelped by society, but I also think *that could have been me,* and, for a long time, it was.

I was invisible to so many people, yet there was an awareness of our family and my situation to some extent. The files clearly state that there were concerns over my 'physical chastisement', that my parents were using me as an outlet when things went wrong between them, and that I was far too knowing, both in terms of being sexually aware and in the way I interacted with adults.

Would anyone have noticed if this had all taken place today rather than more than thirty years ago? I'd like to think so, but I doubt it. Even in a society where there is more talk about child abuse, I'm not sure it can ever be solved. What is clear is that there are still mothers like mine. The ways in which some people can manipulate the system have never changed. She would always represent it as a case of 'us' against 'them', despite never making any attempt to bond with me. I was to tell outsiders nothing, everyone was against us, you stick with your family and that's it. It was a confusing message. I wanted what she was talking about, I wanted our family to be a tight little group that could take on the world, and I would have been happy to shut that world out if she had been a good mum, but she wasn't. One minute she'd be telling me that no one should know anything because they all hated us, then, the next, she'd be telling *me* that she hated me!

Mum would argue with anyone about anything. She could be foul-mouthed and nasty to neighbours and strangers just as much as she was to family. She didn't have any friends, but as far as I could see that was through choice. Mum never seemed to trust anyone or accept that they were being genuine; she always thought they had an agenda. As a result, the attitudes of others towards us weren't just based on what we had done but what they thought we *might* do. We were, in fact, ostracized by the community, but a lot of that (in fact, the vast majority of it) was our own fault. The sad fact was that we had no positive role models at home. Dad was unpredictable and violent, while Mum thought that the world owed her a living. There was nothing positive to hold on to really. When I see children now who are being neglected or left to drag themselves up it breaks my heart because I *know* that if they are like that in public, then their home lives are a hundred times worse. I know because that was *my life*.

My siblings ran wild. I didn't in the same way because I had so many responsibilities. I didn't break windows or scream at the top of my voice as I ran through the streets at that stage (although it would happen later), not because I was any different to them but because I simply didn't have the time. From the age of six, I was given a job by Mum: I began liaising with the authorities. Mum's hatred of talking to anyone who she saw as 'them' – and that included housing officials, social workers, the DHSS, the police and every other official we had links with – was getting worse. She claimed that they judged her, that they thought she was a bad mother – the irony was that they didn't judge her enough because she was, undoubtedly, a terrible mother. She only cared about appearances when it suited her. She would have gone for anyone who suggested that any of her kids were anything other than angels, but she certainly made my life a misery and ensured that never a day went past that she didn't remind me what a burden I was and how much she regretted ever having me.

I'd love to say that there came a point in my childhood when her words simply washed over me, but it never happened. How can a child just get used to the fact that their mother hates them and that she constantly verbalizes that hatred? Of course, no child *should* have to get used to it, but I wish I could have; I wish I could have developed a thick skin, that it would all have rolled off me like water off a duck's back. Instead, the reality was that every insult, every carefully thrown grenade of hate, gave me pain.

I despise you.
I wish you'd never been born.
I wish I'd never had you.
What is the POINT of you?
Why don't you die?
Do you want me to help you die, or are you finally going to do something worthwhile and get on with it yourself?

It was unrelenting. I can't remember a time when Mum didn't say horrible things to me, so I can only assume that she had kept up this barrage since I had been too little to actually know what she was saying. It hurts me to this day but I think that is because I think of the baby, of the little girl I was, and wonder how anyone, let alone a child's own mother, could say such things and act in such a way. I know that Mum had her own demons, but I also know that there are many, many other fine parents who struggle with such challenges (and more) and would never consider taking it out on their children for a second.

So, when I could get a glimmer of hope of happiness from anything, I would seize it with both hands. I remember the first time I was allowed to use the telephone. I was very excited and thought that it was a huge treat. We didn't have a landline at home so the only way we could call other people was by going to the bright-red public phone box a few hundred yards from our house. It always stank of urine and fags; there would generally be a pile of something unidentifiable in the corner (vomit I would think) and the graffiti was so basic that even a six-year-old could read it, even if I didn't understand quite what it was referring to. I had no interest in who was a 'slag' or who was doing what to the various people whose lives were documented in black marker pen on the tiny-paned windows, but I did have an interest in being allowed to make a call.

The phone box usually had some windows smashed out of it. There would be cigarette burns on the black plastic shelf, and the phone directories that hung from wires underneath it were ripped and tattered. It didn't matter – I still wanted to be allowed in there. It was a rite of passage and a terribly grown-up thing to be able to make calls on my own, even if the only person I could think of ringing was my grandma.

One day, Mum threw my coat at me and snarled, 'Come on.' I jumped off the sofa where I had been drawing in a pad, and pulled my threadbare winter coat on as she headed for the door.

'Where are we going, Mum?' I asked, but there was no reply.

Outside, it was cold and a few flakes of snow were swirling around. Mum was walking fast, pushing Mark in a buggy with Alex on his lap, and I tried to keep up with her. I almost bumped into her back as she came to a sudden stop at the phone box. She opened the door and grabbed me by the arm, roughly shoving me in front of her. The smell hit me in a wave as I watched her pull a plastic bag full of coins from her pocket.

'Time you learned something useful,' Mum said to me.

'The phone?' I asked. 'Am I going to get to use the phone?'

'Well, I'm not here to make fucking fairy cakes with you, am I?' she replied. 'Right,' she went on, pulling a small black address book from her other pocket, 'this is what you need to do.' She licked her finger and flicked through the pages. 'Every number you'll need is here.'

'I think I know it,' I told her.

'Know what?'

'Grandma's number. I think I know it already.'

'So?' she asked. 'Why would I care?'

'Aren't we phoning Grandma?' I whispered.

'No, no we're not. You can mess about and pretend to

phone her in your own time – this is important. You're cold, right? Winter's coming, right? Your coat's too small, right?'

I nodded in reply to each of these questions.

'So – we need money,' she told me.

'Are you going to get a job?' I asked. 'Are you phoning someone about a job?'

Mum snorted. 'Don't be stupid. I'm phoning the social.' She paused.

'No, I'm not actually – *you're* phoning the social.'

'The social' was Mum's catch-all phrase for everyone who helped us – or spied on us, as she called it. Whenever she spoke of the giro money or the social workers or the various people she called for help of any sort, it was referred to as 'the social'. It seemed to me that these people were very kind as they helped us out a lot, though I had no concept of what their role really was. But Mum was always complaining that they didn't give us enough, that she always had to go to them with a begging bowl (I didn't know what that was, and used to try to remember whether we actually had one and where it was kept), and that they were always snooping into our business. However, I did need a coat and I was happy that she had realized that – but I couldn't see how I could phone the social. Surely, they wouldn't talk to a little girl like me?

'Look,' she went on, not knowing that I had a million questions for her. 'You pick the phone up and make sure there's a dialling tone, right? Don't go throwing money away. When there is, dial the number – when they pick up, push the money in. And be quick when you're talking to them, we don't have money to burn, so don't yabber a lot of nonsense – no one's interested. Tell them what you want, get them to promise it, then hang up. Now, listen and learn.'

I stood there as she made a call to the social, telling them that I was freezing, that she had spent all our money on feeding us (which was a lie), and that it was on their conscience if I went to school in rags.

After a few minutes, she thrust the phone down in its receiver.

'Bastards,' she hissed.

'Didn't it work, Mum?' I asked. 'Am I not getting a new coat?'

'Of course you are,' she told me, 'they've always got money and we can always get it. They're still bastards, though.'

I couldn't imagine for a moment that I would have the confidence or ability to be like that. I was still only six years old and she was telling me I was going to have to take on bureaucracy. What I should have realized was that when Mum decided something it was a done deal.

We walked home in silence.

'Right,' she said as soon as we got back in. 'Pay attention. This is what you need to do. One – always tell them that I'm too ill or too upset to make the call, but if they ask you if you're being looked after, you'd better bloody make sure they believe that I'm Mother of the Year. Two – always cry, but only *after* you've told them what you want. Three – only tell them the bare minimum. The bastards would love to poke their noses in even more if they could, so don't give them any excuses. Understand?'

I wasn't sure that I did.

Was I going to be making all the calls now? Mum's next words left me in no doubt.

'It's time for you to start making a contribution, do you hear me? It's been take, take, take for far too long. I rue the day I had you, but maybe you can serve some sort of purpose. I'm worn out with trying to make sure we get what we're entitled to, you need to be a grown-up now, Sophie – do you hear me?'

I did.

I was six years old, but it was time for me to step up to the plate. I ended up hating that red box. Phoning wasn't the fun I had thought it would be. Often Mum would decide on the spur of the moment that we needed to make a call so I'd be dragged out in all weathers. Sometimes it was as if she realized that since we were out anyway she may as well make a trip of it, so we'd go to the butcher's or to see one of her other boyfriends. The boys were usually with Grandma when this happened, or Mark would be at pre-school and Alex at nursery, while she kept me off school to do chores or make calls. I remember one time when it must have been quite late as it was getting dark. The boys were already in bed when she came into my room for me, unlocking the door and telling me to come with her.

'Where are we going?' I asked.

'Phone box,' she snapped.

I thought this was odd. It was past the time when I knew the offices of the social would close; the times and numbers were engraved in my mind.

'I don't think there will be anyone there,' I told Mum.

'Shut up, little miss fucking know-it-all,' she replied.

'Do as I tell you – and keep quiet; I don't want to wake Mark and Alex.'

We crept out of the house but when we got to the phone box she kept walking.

'Mum . . .' I began. 'Mum, I don't think they'll be there. It's late, Mum; I think they all go home.'

I *knew* they would all be home. Mum had told me about the places the people from the social lived in. Palaces, she said. They all had posh houses and lovely things, they barely lifted a finger and they got it all on our money. I didn't know how that worked, but I did know that if I lived in a palace I would be home by the time it got dark too.

She stopped and looked at me.

'You're probably right for once, they'll all be off home to their mansions, counting the money they've stolen from me,' she said. 'Still, we're out now, may as well make the most of it.'

We kept walking into town and it seemed that she knew almost every man we passed.

'All right, Jenny?' they would say. 'You out for a bit?'

'Who's this, then?' some of them asked, looking at me. 'Latest recruit?' She'd laugh and flirt while I thought that they were bad men, like the butcher who liked her a lot or like my granddad.

After we had been walking for a little while, we got to a part of town that was close to about three different pubs and a bus stop.

'I need to rest my feet,' she said to me. 'Come and sit here.'

She hopped up on to a wall – it wasn't too high, but she

still needed to help me get up on it. It was the sort where I could swing my legs, which I did, making sure I didn't scrape my legs on the bricks as I had a short dress on. It was getting colder and later, but Mum was being quite nice to me, by her standards, so I didn't feel too bad.

She kept looking along the street and at the pubs as if she was waiting for someone, but when I asked if that was the case she just told me to shut up and stop imagining things. After a while, a man in his twenties came along the street and smiled at Mum. I got the sense that they knew each other and was proved right when he stopped. He said something to Mum, which I thought she must have heard, but, for some reason, she asked me what it was.

'I don't know,' I told her, which was the truth, but I would have said it anyway so that she couldn't accuse me of eavesdropping.

'Listen harder,' she told me.

The man came closer to me this time and I got a knot in my stomach as soon as he spoke.

'If you open your legs, I'll give you a fiver,' he said.

At first, I thought he must be meaning Mum, that he was telling me so that I could tell her, but the leering look on his face and the way she was smiling made me think again.

'What did he say? What did he say?' Mum pressed.

'I'm not sure,' I lied.

'Say it again,' she commanded him.

'If you open your legs, I'll give you a fiver,' he repeated.

I shook my head. It was obvious Mum had heard him this time and I was so embarrassed.

'No! No!' I shouted. My heart was beating very fast and

I wanted to run away, knowing that, unless Mum said I could go, I was stuck there.

'If you open your legs, I'll give you a fiver,' he repeated once more.

I looked at Mum.

She nodded.

'Do it,' she said to me. 'She'll do it,' she said to him.

I shook my head. This was wrong, it was really wrong.

The man put his hand on my leg.

'You do it,' he told me. 'I want you to lift your skirt and open your legs. I've got money.'

Mum kept smiling at me as if this was great fun. Fun. Normal. All the things Granddad tried to convince me his games were too.

I couldn't do it. I started crying.

'Oh for fuck's sake, Jenny,' the man said and walked away.

So, he did know her. It was planned. Mum dragged me off the wall and beat the hell out of me when we got home. For once, it was worth it. Somehow I felt that, if I'd done what she and that man had wanted, I'd have passed a point of no return. I took the blows that night knowing that, appallingly, they were preferable to some of things she wanted for me. I had grown up. I had grown up in the most dreadful fashion that night and I knew without a doubt that Mum thought absolutely nothing of me at all, and it could, I felt, only get worse.

I started to look all around me for evidence of other girls being abused. It never occurred to me that it could happen to boys as well. This was partly because I wanted to see if I was abnormal because I hated it so much, but I also wondered whether it was just something else I was missing. I couldn't understand why Mum hated me and this annoyed me because if I could work it out, I could change, so, similarly, I thought that if I could find out if other girls were being touched and were surrounded by sex, I could see how they coped with it and maybe copy them.

Katy no longer spoke to me at school after the disastrous sleepover at my house. However, another girl had started in my class and we too found ourselves drawn to each other. This girl, Wendy, was from a housing estate close to mine, but the houses there were different. It may have still been an estate but that was where the similarities ended. These homes were newly built, with clean fronts and tidy little gardens that generally contained baskets of flowers. It was like another world. In my mind it was like where the people from the social would live.

Wendy seemed normal. She wasn't fat or smelly, she wasn't skinny or bruised, but there was something about her that marked her out as different, because the other kids kept away from her and she kept away from them. I've often wondered as an adult what the unspoken language is between children that makes them know so much – if social workers and police officers could access that knowledge, they'd probably save thousands of kids in every community. Whatever the reason, Wendy didn't really have friends, despite being pretty and well-dressed. Even more oddly, she gravitated towards me. We were an odd couple. I was unkempt and neglected, smelly and defiant. She was pretty and neat – but we were kindred spirits in some way. We started hanging out together at break time and lunch, and Wendy would share her treats with me.

When she spoke of her mum and dad, it was like another world. Her dad was away a lot too, but with him it was due to his work. When he returned from whatever he did he brought Wendy gifts and she never mentioned anything bad he did. Her mum didn't work, like mine, but that, again, was the only similarity. There was no suggestion from Wendy that she was beaten or abused by them, but there was something wrong, I just knew it.

Wendy had a big sister called Nicola who was about ten years older than us. Nicola was at college and would often be the one to pick Wendy up after school. She would pick her little sister up and seem delighted to see her, and my heart would ache with jealousy when I saw how they were together. Wendy spoke about Nicola all the time, and I hoped that one day Mark and Alex would discuss me with the same level of adoration to their friends.

One day, Wendy asked if I wanted to go to her house after school to play. This was the first time I had ever been invited anywhere. I was beside myself with excitement.

When I asked Mum if I could go, she raised her eyebrows.

'Those posh houses on the new estate?' she asked.

I nodded.

'Someone wants *you* to go there?' She laughed.

I nodded again.

'Good luck to them,' she sniggered. 'It serves the posh bastards right if you piss all over their fancy carpets. I bet your little friend hasn't mentioned it's a darkie she's bringing round for dinner, has she?'

Her words washed over me. I had a friend. I was going to my friend's house. This could be the start of something so normal, so good, that I could barely contain myself.

Wendy and I counted down the days. I had nothing to take with me, but she said that didn't matter; she had plenty of toys. On the day itself, Nicola was waiting for us at the school gate.

'Are you excited, girls?' she asked, smiling.

I was a bit shy around her. I didn't have any experience of ordinary families, and Nicola seemed too much like a grown-up for me to relax completely. She was big, not overweight, but really substantial and physically very different to Wendy.

When we got to Wendy's house, I couldn't believe my eyes. It was clean – but so was my home because of Mum's OCD. The difference here was that there was a real feeling of warmth and homeliness. There were photographs of the two girls everywhere, there were soft cushions and a record player on a sideboard. It was a proper home, not just somewhere to exist while you waited for the next beating.

We played in Wendy's room, where she had so much more than I could ever have imagined, then, after a while, Nicola called us downstairs. She was sitting on a sofa in the living room with a book on her lap.

'Do you fancy a story?' she asked.

'Story, story, story!' Wendy chanted, jumping on to the sofa and planting herself beside her big sister. I remember that Nicola was reading from a large book of fairy tales, and I felt that that was just the sort of world I had wandered into. Nicola patted the sofa at the other side of her and smiled at me.

'Sit here, Sophie,' she said. 'Do you want to choose?'

I picked a page at random and listened to the tale. I sat intently at Nicola's side as she read, but Wendy was on her lap, cuddling in. After a while, I noticed that Nicola was quietly tickling her little sister. I thought of all the times I had to put up with tickling that meant something else and my mind wandered off the story for a while. When I pulled myself back again, everything had changed. Nicola was still tickling Wendy – but this was the sort of tickling I knew far too well. Her hands were all over her sister, and Wendy's skirt was up round her waist. I saw the older girl's hand dart inside the knickers of my friend and I felt sick. It was happening here too. It was happening everywhere.

'Come here, Sophie!' said Nicola, trying to pull me towards her. I veered away, but she grabbed me quickly.

'Come on! Let's have fun!' she said.

There were no other grown-ups in the house, and it was very clear to me that Wendy was used to this sort of 'fun' with her big sister. I didn't want it. Was this my punishment, I wondered. Was this my punishment for trying to persuade Katy that what Dad wanted was fine? It must have been, because now Wendy was trying to encourage me.

'Go on!' she said. 'Let Nicola tickle you, Sophie!'

She was laughing her head off as the older girl touched her all over. She didn't seem scared, she just seemed to find it all perfectly everyday.

'No,' I whispered. 'No.'

As the two girls did whatever they were doing on the sofa in that perfect house, I left. The image of Nicola abusing her own little sister was in my mind as I walked back to my home.

I had been looking for evidence that abuse was everywhere and now that I had found it, I was sickened. If it could happen in that environment, with a good mummy and daddy, with love and everything material you could wish for, what chance did I have?

Just as Katy and I had never spoken again, it was now all ruined with Wendy. I felt as if everything around me was tainted and that nothing was free of sex. If nice, good, perfect girls like Wendy were never taken out of those sorts of situations, what hope was there for someone like me, someone so horrible, so unlovable, so disgusting that even my own mother hated me? None. None at all.

When I got home, Mum was on the sofa with one of her boyfriends while the boys played on the floor. She stopped kissing whatever man it was just long enough to notice I was there.

'Oh, Christ, are you back already?' she asked. 'What happened? Did you piss yourself? Shit on their carpets? Make them sick looking at your face?' She laughed at her own fantastic sense of humour.

'Probably,' I said, walking towards my room. 'Probably.'

Chapter 7

Are you still here?

Sophie is under a lot of pressure, has run off and
drunk aftershave in the last month. I'm seeing the
family regularly. I'm not anticipating further
dangerous behaviour from Sophie.
Social work files 4325G/
Sophie Gilmore

When I was seven Mum found a new way to make my life
a misery. Although I was still only little, she treated me like
an adult in that she spoke about inappropriate things and
hit me with the force of someone who thought their victim was the same size as them. But, from that point, she
ramped things up a notch.

'You ever thought of killing yourself, Sophie?' she
asked casually one day as she sat in a chair, bouncing Alex
on her knee while Mark played on the floor nearby.

I looked at her with my big brown eyes, not knowing
how to respond.

'Well, have you?' she went on. 'Ever thought of putting

us all out of our misery and topping yourself? It'd be the best thing all around, don't you think? ANSWER ME!' she shouted.

'No – no I haven't,' I said in a little voice.

'Well, you are thick, I suppose. Never mind, now that I've given you the idea, don't you think it's about time?'

Mum sat and watched me from the sofa. I didn't have many toys, but I was playing with a dolly on the rug in front of the fire.

After about five minutes she said, 'Why are you still here?'

I ignored her. I didn't know what to say – where would I go?

'I said, why the fuck are you still here?' she snarled.

When she snarled, it took over her whole face. She gritted her teeth, and pulled her eyebrows down tight on her forehead. I felt scared. She actually looked evil to me. I was used to these words. I knew they were bad and I should never say them, but I heard them so much that I sometimes ignored them. She wasn't going to let me get away with that today.

'Did you not hear me? Are you fucking deaf now?' she asked.

'I heard you, Mummy,' I whispered.

'Then answer me. WHY ARE YOU STILL FUCK-ING HERE?'

How could I? How could a seven-year-old answer that?

She was always so angry and so cold, and those types of 'conversations' coloured my early years. There were days when the only words she'd say to me were hateful ones. I knew why she was saying it, because she told me. She had told me so many times that the wrong daughter had died, that she wished it had been me and not Fiona. It was as if she had a selection of phrases she would use every day and they all sent the same message – she hated me and I was worthless.

Why are you here?

Why aren't you dead?

Do you know why I hate you?

Why couldn't you be the one who died?

Are you going to die soon?

Can you hurry up and die?

You fucking horrible disgusting child . . . I HATE HATE HATE YOU.

This became her new thing. She would ask me every day how I was getting on with my plans to kill myself. The only time I saw her smile was when she asked me that.

We were struggling financially so Mum often took us all to her parents' house. She told me it was my fault that we had no money, that I wasn't getting enough from the social and I believed her. When we went to Grandma and Granddad's, Mum would make us all eat as much as possible and take lots away with us too for later on. Despite how she had reacted to my mum and treated her when she had announced her first pregnancy, Grandma loved me now and I was secure in that knowledge at least. Grandma still worked, as an office manager, and Granddad was a signalman on the railways, having previously had a job as a prison officer after he had come out of the Army.

Sometimes when I was with Granddad he told me

stories that confused me. He told me that when he had worked in a prison, keeping the bad men locked up, some of those bad men had done terrible things to children just like me.

'There are men who touch little girls all over,' he'd say. 'Bad men. They touch them in their knickers, they touch their private parts. These men are horrible men. They get locked up. They get put in prison and everyone hates them. Isn't the world a terrible place, Sophie? Touching little girls right inside their knickers . . .'

I didn't know what to say.

These were the things Granddad did to me. Was he warning me that other men would want to do these things to me? Did he know about Dad, I wondered. Was he telling me that he would go to prison if anyone found out, and that he would be the one everyone hated? I was so bewildered. I wanted to tell someone what Granddad was doing to me because I didn't like it, but I was caught between a rock and a hard place. They would either not believe me and I'd be punished, maybe kept away from Grandma forever, or they would believe me, and my granddad would go to prison. I was torn in the way that so many abused children are. I didn't want my abuser to be jailed, or even to get into trouble; I just wanted it to stop. I wanted him to be the sort of grandfather who loved me without the touching or looking at my knickers, I didn't want him to be shouted at by the police and then put into a jail, like the one he used to work in.

I loved it at Grandma's house when I could keep away from Granddad and his confusing words and horrible actions. By now, I hated home. I could never please Mum, everything I did annoyed her, and she spewed bile at me at every chance she got. No matter what I did, it was wrong and she resented me. She'd flash me that look of hate and remind me again that the wrong child had survived.

I never went near Dad. I was frightened of him by now as he'd started hitting me too. I could never relax when he was there. Mum hated me, but she didn't attack me the way he did. He was still hitting her regularly, but he'd moved on to me too. The irony was that there were always social workers around the place. Due to her obsessive-compulsive disorder the house was always clean and tidy. She would fly off the handle if I made any mess at all – even leaving the lids off pens when I was drawing – but the social workers only saw what they wanted. A clean house meant they could tick a box, but they never opened their eyes to the type of life I was really living; they only cared that the place was dusted and smelled of furniture polish.

Dad's anger was still coming out of nowhere on the rare occasions he was there. He'd whack me on my bare bum with slippers so often that my only response would be to run off to the kitchen afterwards to get some margarine to rub into it, which would soothe the pain a little. He was acting strangely. While his anger and violence had always been constant, he was also overeating to a huge extent. I was aware of people laughing at him and calling him even more names than usual as he lost his good looks and became a figure of fun where we lived. I don't know what size he was then, but I do remember going shopping with Mum at around that time: we'd had to buy him size fifty-four trousers.

By the time I was seven, my life had settled into a routine of mental worry, abuse, physical beatings and emotional coldness. I was continuing to scan things, to look for clues of when it might all go wrong, but, to be honest, it was always wrong.

Dad was still disappearing for weeks at a time, but no one ever told me where he went. Sometimes when he came back, he would bring me a gift – some strawberry bonbons, my favourite sweets, and, once, a red butterfly brooch that I adored. He would be nice to me for a little while, but Mum would hate that and stand behind me snarling whenever he paid me any positive attention.

My little girl is now the same age as I was then. She's my last baby, my one girl in a gang of four boys. I adore them all, but this little girl, my Daisy, has changed my world. I look at her and love pours out of me. I want to protect her forever. I want to keep her safe and make sure no one ever harms her. I want to do all the things for her that no one ever did for me. When I think back to what it was like for me then, and I look at how small and vulnerable she is, I can hardly breathe. It seems incredible. My mother didn't see me as a daughter, she just saw me as someone to hate. If Daisy had no love in her life, I struggle to think of how she would cope. But I did. I had to.

Mum would often say her most hateful things while she was hugging Mark and Alex; it was as if she wanted to emphasize to me just *how much* she hated me, and *how much* she loved them.

She fell pregnant again after Alex, and, this time, she told me about it.

'I've got another filthy little darkie bastard in my belly,' she hissed at me one day. 'Never mind, this one's not getting a chance to torment me – just my luck it would be like you.'

I stared at her because I never knew how to respond when she started telling me things that weren't really suitable for a child to hear. It was as if I was someone to offload on to, rather than a daughter to love and care for.

'Your dad's sorting it out,' she went on. 'He's not kicking this one out of me, oh no. We're going all medical this time and my lovely, caring husband has me booked in for an abortion tomorrow – isn't that nice? Do you like the idea of your little sister or brother being sucked out of me, kicking and screaming, do you?'

She didn't want me to answer, and, of course, I couldn't. I remember not understanding much of what she was saying, but the next day we did go to stay with Grandma. And the next. When we arrived back home with Grandma Mum was already there, cleaning the kitchen.

'Are you all right, Jennifer?' asked Grandma.

'Always am,' came the reply.

'Maybe it's for the best,' I remember Grandma saying.

Although she must have been telling her own mother, Mum crouched down and hissed in my face instead. 'Well, it won't fucking happen again, will it? He's made me have my fucking tubes tied. No more babies for me.'

This was something I did have an answer to. Mum hated me so it must be good news if she wasn't going to have any more little girls, mustn't it?

'That's nice, Mummy,' I said.

'Unbelievable,' she said. 'Fucking unbelievable.'

'She's just a child, Jenny,' said my grandma. 'She doesn't know what she's saying – you shouldn't be talking to her like that anyway.'

'Oh, she knows what she's saying,' replied Mum. 'She knows how to twist the knife, that one.

If I did, I'd learned at the hands of a master. There was never any softness to her as far as I was concerned.

'Are you still fucking here?' she'd shout out of nowhere. 'Get out of my fucking house, get out!'

The first time she said that, I thought she was joking – but she wasn't. She shoved me to the door and opened it. 'Go on, I've had enough of you, get the fuck out of my house.'

She slammed the door behind me. I was seven, it was raining and my own mother had kicked me out. I stood there for a while then wandered around the estate. There was nothing for me to do. I didn't have any friends, so there were no other houses I could go to. The kids who were playing outside shouted, 'Look, it's the stinky Paki!' I headed for the phone box so that it looked like I had a purpose, somewhere to go. When I got there, I pretended to myself that I was going to phone Grandma, that all I was doing was organizing a sleepover. I pretend to dial and spoke into an empty receiver. When it was over, I felt just as empty myself.

I wandered back home, dreading what would meet me there, but not knowing what else I could possibly do. Mum was in her room when I got back and didn't say anything to me for the rest of that night.

It became a pattern.

She'd tell me to 'Get out of my fucking sight, get out of my fucking house,' and I'd just go. It was easier that way. If I walked for a little bit, there was a big park with massive fields nearby and I could spend some time there. I had always scanned for safe places ever since I was tiny, and the slide in the play park was one of the places I had thought of. I believed that if the park was empty, I'd be safe there. One night, when I was in bed, Mum came into my room shouting and screaming.

'WHY are you still here? WHY have you not killed yourself?' she screeched. 'OUT! OUT! OUT!' she yelled, dragging the covers off me and pulling me out of bed. She got hold of my wrists and hauled me to the door, still in my nightclothes. I was thrown outside and the door slammed behind me. 'KILL YOURSELF! KILL YOUR-SELF NOW!' I heard Mum shriek.

I got up and made my way to the play park. It was the middle of the night, so it was totally deserted. I climbed up the steps to the top of the slide. That freezing cold slide in the middle of an empty park at two o'clock in the morning felt a whole lot safer than my own bed-room. I was frightened, but I was away from her. There would be no beatings that night and that was worth stay-ing out for.

I lasted a couple of hours and then went to one of our neighbours, a woman called Mrs Nicolson. I knew that Mum hated her because she was always complaining about us. There was something about her that I liked, though – maybe just the fact that she took the time to complain, rather than ignore everything, which was what most of the neighbours ended up doing after constantly listening to the Gilmores day in and day out.

I knocked at her door and waited for ages. I had to try a few times before she finally answered it. Her eyes nearly popped out of her head when she saw me.

'What the hell are you doing here at this time of the morning?' she asked.

'I've run away,' I said. It was almost the truth.

'Have you now?' she replied. 'You best come in then. Sophie, isn't it?' she queried, closing the door behind me.

'Yes,' I told her. 'How do you know my name?'

She snorted.

'I've heard your mother screaming it at you enough times to have it burned in my memory. Run away, have you?'

I nodded.

She looked at me with penetrating eyes.

'Well . . . Mum kicked me out,' I admitted.

'She what? She kicked you out? What age are you?' she asked.

'Seven.'

'She kicked out a seven-year-old?'

I nodded again.

'In the middle of the night?'

I nodded another time.

Mrs Nicolson sighed and shook her head.

'That bloody woman. She's not fit to be a mother. Now, let's get you warmed up and into bed,' she smiled, taking my hand and leading me to the kitchen. She heated up some milk and gave me a biscuit, before showing me into what was obviously a guest room. I knew Mrs Nicolson lived alone and it didn't look as if she'd had a visitor in a long time. The bed was piled high with cushions and pillows. I sank into it gratefully.

I think I'd slept for a few hours before I was woken by someone shaking my shoulder. For a terrible moment, I thought I was at home and Dad was back but it was someone else – it was a policeman.

'Sophie?' he said gently. 'Sophie – Mrs Nicolson says you've run away from home?'

'No – no, I didn't say that,' the woman interrupted. 'I told you that poor little mite has a waste of space for a mother, more interested in throwing herself at men than looking after her kids, and that she'd chucked that child out. What are you going to do about it?'

The policeman hustled Mrs Nicolson out of the room. I must have fallen asleep again for a little while because I remember him shaking my arm, just like before.

'Right, Sophie,' he said. 'Let's get you back to your mum.'

I said nothing – but I saw Mrs Nicolson's face, looking as if she was furious by how things were working out.

'You're taking her back?' she spat. 'You're taking that child back to the place she was kicked out of?'

'We've no choice,' the policeman said. 'She needs to be returned home.'

Sleepily, I got out of the bed and took his hand. He put me in the back of the police car even though we were driving barely any distance at all. When he knocked on our door, Mum acted as if she had been going mad with worry.

'Where have you been? Oh God, I was out of my mind!'

She thanked the policeman profusely and said that she'd keep an even closer eye on me, telling him that she didn't know what had got into me, that my dad had recently upset me, that I was a very emotional child – all sorts of things that seemed to put his mind at rest. Then, as soon as the door was closed on him, all hell broke loose.

'You stupid, stupid little bitch!' she yelled. 'If you leave this house, you make fucking sure that you leave it forever – you do the job, do you hear me? You do the job and get yourself run over or taken away, or something, anything, that makes sure I never, NEVER have to see your fucking face ever again.'

There was a moment when I first came back when I wondered if the words she was saying to the policeman were true. Maybe she had missed me, perhaps she had been worried. They were the things a concerned mummy should say, but, as the blows rained down on me afterwards, I was reminded, yet again, that this was what she thought of me. This was the real her, when she was with me. I was thrown from one room to the other, completely unable to go to school the next day once again.

My files say:

Inspector X thought of taking her to a place of safety but was advised by social workers not to do so. Contact has been difficult to establish. I believe Sophie is at risk as she has been truanting – she has also been reported wandering around at all times of the day and night.

I wish that police officer had stood his ground and made sure that I was placed under an order to take me away. It's hard to believe that he wanted that, that they knew I was at risk, that my truanting was established, that I'd been seen wandering around day and night, and that they admitted they found it difficult to establish contact with Mum – yet I was still left there.

The day after I had been brought home by the police (only a few hours later really), Mum came into my room smiling. She didn't sniff the sheets or start shouting like she usually did, she simply drew the curtains back and came over to me as I drowsily sat up.

'Here you go, Sophie, this is for you,' she said, handing me a kitchen knife.

I stared at her. I wasn't allowed knives; they were dangerous. 'Time for you to do it, don't you think? Stick this in – you won't feel a thing. Go on, do it.'

She handed me the knife and I held it, terrified, as she continued to smile. The awful thing was, I wanted to die. I did, I wanted to die – but I didn't want to hurt myself. I knew she was lying, it definitely would hurt to insert that shiny steel blade into myself, no matter which part of my body I chose. I was scared. I didn't want my life to be like this, and I also, bizarrely, wanted to please her, so I would have done it – I would have tried to kill myself if I could have been sure it wouldn't hurt, but surely that wasn't an option with a blade?

Maybe I could try?

I put the knife to my stomach, and her smile got even wider.

I pressed – but only gently. I was so scared of what it would be like, and I couldn't continue.

'Try harder,' Mum said.

I couldn't work out what to do. How could I possibly be brave enough to stick that knife into my stomach knowing how much it would hurt, despite what she said? Then I had an idea. Maybe I could do it not by moving the knife, but by moving me. Mum would be happy with me then, wouldn't she? Not only would I have hurt myself, killed myself maybe, but I would also have worked out the problem so she wouldn't think I was so stupid any more.

Suddenly, I had a brainwave.

I moved all the pillows and shoved them into a pile. I pushed all my bedding round the pillows, then I wedged the knife into the middle, blade sticking upwards, into the air. Now all I had to do was lay myself on it. If I positioned my stomach above the knife I would just have to lower myself on to it – gently if I stayed scared, quickly if I got brave – and it would happen. I'd have done it.

Mum's eyes were shining brightly as she watched me, a smile playing about her lips.

'Go on,' she whispered. 'Do it. Do it.'

I had to press my hands and my feet on to the bed at the same time so that I was the shape of a crab. My tummy hovered above the blade and I could hear her say 'Do it' over and over again beside me. I closed my eyes and pushed myself slowly on to the knife; I couldn't do it quickly.

In fact, I couldn't do it at all. As soon as I felt it push

into the softness of my body, I also felt the trickle of warm blood that appeared. I felt faint, dizzy – I knew the blood was mine and I knew it would get much worse if I continued.

'Do it,' Mum said. 'Do it.'

Crying, I threw myself to the side as the blood soaked the sheets.

'I can't Mum, I can't!' I wept, sobbing uncontrollably. 'I'm so sorry, I really am.'

All I could think of was how disappointed she would be that I'd failed again.

'You useless little fucker,' she snarled, the shine gone from her eyes. I leaned over and took the knife out from its wedged position in the pillows, threw it to the floor and Mum clattered me across the head.

'Fucking useless,' she snapped, walking away.

It was as if the night that I had been thrown out had increased Mum's desire to get rid of me. A few days after the knife incident we were in the living room. She was on the sofa at the other end of the room from me, staring at me silently.

'Strangle yourself,' she said eventually, calmly. 'Go on, do it.'

'No, Mummy,' I whispered. 'No.'

'You'll fucking do it,' she said. She took off the belt she was wearing, one of those stretchy ones that had a clip on either end that joined up when it was closed. 'Use this. Do it now. Do it now, Sophie.'

She handed the belt to me.

'Put it round your neck. Do it.'

I took the belt from her and made a tentative move to

place it round my neck. I wanted to please her, wanted to die, but I just couldn't do it.

'I can't, Mum,' I cried. 'I can't.'

'You fucking stupid bastard!' she screamed. Hitting, kicking, pulling my hair, nipping – all this went on in front of my little brother, all because I couldn't kill myself. I wanted it to end but I couldn't do what she wanted me to do.

So, I'd do other things.

I'd take medicine.

I'd go to the cupboard and take a bottle of medicine.

I'd say, 'Look, Mum, look what I'm doing for you.'

I'd drink whatever was left in the bottle as she watched.

When I'd finished, she'd walk off as if I'd done nothing. I did that on plenty of occasions and got nothing more than a tummy ache, or sometimes I'd be sick from what I'd gulped down to please her.

She just wanted me dead – and she wanted me to do it to myself. She was happy to beat me up, but I would have to take the final step myself.

Mum had fluid for cleaning rings in a blue bottle. It was pink, bright pink, and she kept it in her room.

'Why don't you try this?' she said one day. 'You've been fucking useless with everything else, maybe this will work.'

She handed me the bottle and wafted it under my nose. The most disgusting smell came out of it.

'I think,' Mum said in a very measured voice, 'that this might do the trick. It smells horrible, doesn't it, Sophie? Just imagine what it'll taste like – rather you than me, but let's see, shall we? Let's see if we can finally get you sorted out.'

I took the bottle from her as she stared at me.

I put it to my lips and forced myself to drink some. She was right; it was absolutely hideous. It was like drinking petrol, I thought. I started throwing up almost immediately and as I vomited, she kicked me. Every time I was sick, she shouted at me to drink more. I was hardly taking any of it in, I think I was being sick because of my gag reflex more than anything, but she was furious. I wasn't dead and that angered her so much.

I spent a lot of time trying to work out if there was a way I could kill myself that wouldn't hurt. That was the terrible mindset I was in. One day, Mum was lying on her bed, doing nothing, and the boys were playing around the house. I went in to see what she was up to and she turned a blank gaze on me.

My eyes scanned her room and saw a jar of pins.

'Would you like me to eat these, Mum?' I asked solemnly. 'Shall I eat the pins for you?'

She said nothing.

'I think they'll hurt – would you like that?'

Again, silence.

I walked out of the room. I would only do it if she was going to be happy. If she didn't even notice, there was no point.

Every day, I heard the same things from Mum:

You've been nothing but trouble.

You make my life a misery.

I wish I'd never had you.

You bring trouble to this house.

She was right; I was acting up by the time I was seven, going on for eight. I was smashing windows and I was causing a lot of trouble. Mum hated her neighbours because they were always complaining about her, so I thought if I caused bother to them, she'd love me. I broke their windows, turned over their rubbish bins, stole their washing, anything I could think of, and still she didn't love me. To try to please her, I went on the rampage, but it still did nothing.

Once when she was in the kitchen feeding my brothers, I saw a bottle of washing-up liquid at the side of the sink.

'Shall I drink that? Shall I drink that, Mum?' I asked.

'If you like – but keep it away from my boys,' she said. 'I don't want anything happening to them.'

I started swallowing the green liquid. It was vile and I couldn't manage much. I took a drink to take the taste away and in the hope that I could manage more, but all that happened was that bubbles started coming out of my mouth.

Mum, Mark and Alex began hooting with laughter.

I was crying, trying to poison myself, and they were in fits of hysterics.

'Would you look at your stupid sister?' Mum said to them. 'What a thick bitch!'

They all laughed and laughed and laughed as the tears ran down my cheeks. I was running out of ideas. Mum was spending a lot of time in her bedroom, Dad wasn't around, and there were no boyfriends at the moment. My mind went back to the jar of pins. As the thought of swallowing them filled me with horror, I thought that it must be a good idea – if it was something I'd hate to do, if it was something that would cause me pain, then surely

Mum would like it? And, if she liked what I did, maybe she would like me.

I picked the container up yet again.

'I could swallow these if you wanted me to, Mum. Shall I? Shall I swallow them?'

She nodded and my heart lifted at her reaction.

They were tiny little pins, the sort that dressmakers use. I wasn't sure how they'd go down my throat. I needed a drink, but I knew I had to ask permission, just as I had to ask permission for everything.

'Can I get some water, please?' I asked.

'Whatever,' she replied, as if I was preparing for the most boring thing in the world. I walked to the kitchen and came back with a beaker of cold water.

I sat on her bed with the jar of pins and the drink, and started swallowing them one by one. I have no idea how I did it. I think I swallowed over fifty of them, and she couldn't have cared less. Nothing happened to me.

'You're fucking stupid,' she hissed. 'You can't even fucking kill yourself. Fuck off.'

Looking back, I have no idea how I managed to escape from all the things I ate and drank. Maybe cough medicine isn't as poisonous as the labels say, maybe they exaggerate so that good mummies and daddies are extra-careful. The people who make the medicine aren't likely to put a label on saying, *If you want your child to die, make sure they use something else; this won't work.* Maybe the pins just all came out when I went to the toilet.

Or maybe there was a reason for me to survive it all – that's the best thought I can have, because when I think about the hell of it, I can barely breathe. I have to think there was a purpose to my survival.

She hated me – and I hated me.

I was useless. I knew that from a very young age. I hated being there but I couldn't kill myself. I had to live that life because I was too little to think of an effective means of suicide.

I was a terrible child because I couldn't kill myself – that was the sum total of my life.

Chapter 8

Games afternoon

To Child Abuse Committee:
Please be advised that meetings about Sophie
Gilmore are informal, not full investigations.
Social work files 4325G/
Sophie Gilmore

The social-work files that state I had swallowed aftershave are quite unusual in that they record that at all. Of course, I had swallowed much more than that, but I remember telling them about the aftershave, and the aftershave alone, because I was at the doctor so much with stomach pains. I was drinking so many horrible things that it was no wonder I was having digestive problems, but I never told anyone in authority the full extent of it.

I can't remember exactly what it was that I had swallowed that made the pains so bad that Mum took me to the GP, but it must have been pretty bad as she usually avoided anyone official. I know I was doubled up in agony and had been vomiting for a few days when she finally announced, 'For fuck's sake – I suppose I'll have to drag you to the doctor before you stop being such a bloody drama queen.'

'She's got stomach pains – or so she says,' Mum told the doctor. 'I don't know what to do with her,' she continued, trying to look concerned. 'It's one thing after another – go on, Sophie, tell the nice man how you feel.'

Telling the nice man that I had a sore tummy wasn't enough. He wanted to know how long I'd had it for, had it been there at any other time and had I eaten anything new.

Mum was nodding at me, but I didn't know whether she was telling me to say the truth or not. I decided to give the doctor a version of it in the hope that he could make the pain go away.

'I drank something,' I told him quietly.

'Mmm,' he pondered, poking my tummy. 'Too much fizzy pop?'

I shook my head.

'No – that wouldn't give you this sort of pain for such a long time. So, what did you drink, Sophie?'

I thought for a moment, remembering that I was to blame Dad for everything whenever I could.

'Aftershave,' I told him. 'Dad left his aftershave lying out and I drank that.'

'Oh! Oh!' said Mum dramatically. 'Oh, Sophie, you'll be the death of me, what a worry you are, and what was your father thinking of leaving aftershave lying around where a child could get it?'

'Now, don't worry, Mrs Gilmore,' the doctor said, as she continued to act flustered and concerned. 'It's unlikely to have done any harm. When did you drink it, Sophie?'

'A few days ago,' I told him.

'Well, there we are then,' he concluded. 'If there were to be any serious repercussions, you'd be in hospital by now, young lady. Now, you can see just how concerned your poor mother is, so I want you to promise that you won't get up to any of these antics again.'

I nodded solemnly.

'Thank you so much, doctor,' Mum said flirtily as he handed her a prescription. 'I'm so glad we came to you and it's all over.'

'It's not quite over, Mrs Gilmore,' he told her. 'I see from the files that Sophie has a social worker involved in her case – this will have to be reported, you know.'

Mum was temporarily blindsided.

'Are you sure?' she asked. 'I mean . . . really . . . it's just a little girl being silly . . . we wouldn't want to waste any-one's time.'

'No, this is important,' he replied. 'Sophie may be a danger to herself and this incident has to be logged.'

As soon as we had left the surgery, Mum clattered me on the head.

'Stupid, stupid, stupid . . .' she muttered and I think she meant herself as much as me this time.

What strikes me is that, in another report just a few days after the one that admits I've been drinking toxic things, it says:

we do not anticipate any problems with Sophie . . .

I have no idea how those two things were reconciled by the people who were supposedly looking out for me. I was drinking all sorts – I'd only admitted to one thing – and I was being 'watched' by about six different agencies. How could they not have anticipated any problems? I was a problem just waiting to happen.

When I think back, I realize that I was a very confused little girl on every level. I loved my Grandma so much. She was who I went to when I needed to escape, but what I needed was someone to free me, to see what was going on and take action – not to tell some child-abuse committee that all discussions were informal and that problems were not anticipated. The problems were already happening; the abuse was already ongoing!

When I knew I was going to Grandma's house, with or without my brothers, I was always happy about one thing. I anticipated how lovely my grandma would be, how she would hug me and tell me I was her darling girl. I had looked forward to playing games with my granddad and hearing his stories about what things had been like when he was little, but I now knew there was a price to pay for that.

After he started to touch me, it didn't change things for a while because I could compartmentalize it (although I was too young to realize that was what I was doing). I still loved him, but I didn't want him to do 'those things'. I still wanted to be with him, but not if he was going to do 'those things'. I thought of him as two grandfathers in my head – the one who did 'those things' and the one who did not. And, for a while, I could hope that each visit would be free of the stuff that upset me hugely – but the problem was that I was left alone with him so often. Mum never wanted to stay in when she went to visit her parents. She would no sooner have taken her coat off than she'd be putting it back on again. There was always some excuse to go to the shops or she'd suggest to Grandma that she was feeling lucky and they ought to go to the afternoon bingo session in town. Grandma wasn't always that keen. Her kitchen was well-stocked, she rarely needed anything, she liked to rest in her own home when she wasn't working, and she liked to spend time with me, but Mum was persistent and often got her own mother to give in.

Now that Granddad had started to find ways to entertain himself when we were alone, he was Mum's new advocate, always giving her some money and implying that she should go and treat herself.

'There you go, Jenny,' he'd say, pressing some notes into her hand. 'You look like you could do with cheering yourself up; get your mother to take you into the shops and buy yourself something pretty.'

'Thanks, Dad!' Mum would say, grabbing the coat that had only just been thrown on to the sofa moments before. She'd head to the kitchen where Grandma was usually making up a plate of nice things for me and I'd hear them argue about whether to go out or not. Mum always won. Even when Grandma tried to dig her heels in she'd appear in the living room carrying a tray piled high with cakes and drinks and little crustless sandwiches, only to have Granddad launch into his campaign for her to go out.

'Give me that!' he'd laugh, taking the tray from her. 'That'll see me and little Sophie all right for five minutes! Now, off you go with our Jennifer – I'll look after this one. Take your time, have a girl's day, and I don't want to see you back here before teatime. I mean it! Off you go, enjoy yourselves.'

Grandma would try to protest, but he made it seem very good-natured, so she would, invariably, give in.

'Can't you stay?' I'd ask quietly.

I was really directing the question at my grandma, but it would be Mum who would answer first.

'Give me some peace!' she'd reply. 'I'm with you lot morning, noon and bloody night. The only chance I get is when your dad takes the others once in a blue moon and your granddad looks after you, so don't start bloody moaning.'

'Leave her with me,' he always said. 'I need to just stay in my own house after that last shift. We'll have a games afternoon. We'll have a lovely time, won't we?'

No! I wanted to scream. *No, we won't! It'll be horrible and you'll touch me and I'll smell those horrible smells on you and you'll make me touch you and . . . no! Take me with you!*

I couldn't say any of it. No one would believe me and Mum would make me pay a hundred times over when we got home. Although what Granddad was doing to me was horrible, there was an end point. Nothing ever ended with Mum. I was with her every day, and she never seemed to tire of being horrible to me. If I gave her another reason to hate me – and I did think that it must be my fault that she disliked me so intensely – then I couldn't imagine the level of psychological and emotional pain, let alone physical, that she would inflict on me.

'I'll teach her to play Monopoly,' said Granddad one afternoon as they headed off.

I still remember him saying those words. They would

become his code. I hate Monopoly. I can't play it but I still hate it. I know lots of people say that, they joke about how they get bored by how long it takes or how it always ends up in family fights. But I'm not joking. I hate it. From that very first time that Granddad said he would teach me to play it, I would shake when I heard the word. Even now, when I pass a shop and I see the box, it acts as a trigger. At Christmas, it's everywhere. There are so many versions and my own children have often asked for it, asked for the type that fits in with whatever their obsession is at that moment, whether it's Star Wars or SpongeBob SquarePants or something else. I've never bought it for them, never allowed it to be in the house, because the memories for me are horrendous.

The first day Granddad took it down from a shelf in the mahogany display cabinet in their living room I had no idea that this innocent game was going to have such significance in my childhood. Just as I had always wanted to make telephone calls and now hated that, I had always wanted to play this complicated game that grown-ups never seemed to have any patience for. The box was battered, covered in red, white and black print, and not terribly interesting really. The things that drew me were inside. There were fat batches of money and a little calico bag that held the silver figures. Another bag, plastic this time, contained the hotels and houses. Sometimes I was allowed to play with these, but I had never been given the silver tokens or money before. That was what I wanted, and so when Granddad suggested that we play I was delighted. While previous visits had always ended up with him touching me, I was hopeful that this one would be different. This one would, I was sure, just be about teaching me to play this wonderful game.

He pulled a small table over to the sofa where I had been sitting and perched on the edge of the cushion beside me as he opened the box.

'See?' he said, patting my knee. 'This'll be fun – I'll look after you.'

'Can I count the money, Granddad?' I asked. I couldn't really count that well, but I was desperate to hold the multi-coloured paper with the numbers on. The game itself wasn't that important; I was drawn to all the things that came with it.

'Is that what you want?' he asked.

I nodded.

'Is that the bit you want most?'

I thought about it. It was a big choice to make.

'Well . . .' I considered the options. 'Can I see the silver things too?'

'Of course you can!' he replied. 'In time. All in good time. Now, let's work out what you really want to do – can you tell me?'

I went through the list that was already in my head: I wanted to jiggle the silver tokens in my hand, put the money into colour-coded piles and make a pretend city with the plastic hotels and houses.

'That's a lot!' he laughed, 'but I'm sure that, if you're a good girl, we can manage it.'

He laid everything out on the table and moved a little closer.

'Can we play now?' I asked.

'Almost, almost,' he answered. 'It's just . . . well, it's a bit hot in here and I'm worried that maybe it's not a day for playing Monopoly after all. Maybe you'd be better playing outside.'

It may have been stuffy indoors with the gas fire on and the windows closed, but it was cold outside and I had no wish at all to be playing out there on my own when the alternative was to be in here with my hands on that paper money.

'No, no I'm fine,' I told him. 'Really, I'd rather be here.'

'Are you sure?' he asked. 'I wouldn't want your mum and grandma to come back and think I hadn't been look-ing after you properly. Tell you what – I think you're too wrapped up there; why don't you take some of your things off?'

I stood up, wedged between the sofa and the table, and started to remove my cardigan, but heard him say, 'No, no,' then I felt his hands go up my skirt and pull my knick-ers down.

'Granddad!' I exclaimed. 'Why are you doing that?'

'I told you,' he said calmly. 'It's far too warm in here.'

I reached down and tried to get my pants, which were now lying on the floor but he dragged me back up.

'Do you want to play Monopoly or not?' he enquired.

'Yes, yes I do,' I answered, confused and a bit worried that he could see my bottom.

'Well, stop your nonsense then.'

I wasn't up to any nonsense, I thought. I looked at the game on the table. It wouldn't hurt to do what he said, I thought. When I was sitting down again, I could just pull my skirt over my bum and get on with the game.

'OK,' I whispered.

Granddad had other ideas. He pulled me over to him and manoeuvred me on to his lap. His hands rested on the top of my legs to begin with but they never seemed to stay still.

I learned something that day – everything had a price. Each silver piece had a price, as did the hotels and houses and money. The transactions had nothing to do with Monopoly money and we never did play the game. That horrible old man held up each game piece as if it was a diamonds. If I wanted to touch it, he touched me *there*. When he said I could play with the money from the pretend bank I had to do it while still on his lap, bent over towards the table and wishing the earth would swallow me up as I knew I had no knickers on and I knew he was looking at me, staring at every part of my private areas.

I didn't want to play. I hated the game already, but the fear of him telling Mum that I had been bad, that I hadn't done what I was told, and knowing that she would never believe me if I reported what had happened, was enough to keep me playing his sick version.

Just like the real game, it went on for hours – and I wished to God that I would never see that red and white box for as long as I lived.

He had also started to get me to touch him. It wasn't enough for him to rub himself up and down on me; he wanted me to touch *that* as well.

'Go on, Sophie,' he said one day, 'have a feel of that.'

Again, it was presented as normal; as a treat even.

I tried to avoid it, I showed him my knickers, I even thought of something new to do.

'Look, Granddad!' I said, 'I'm a really good dancer!'

I tried to distract him by dancing around the room for him. I twirled about, knowing that my dress would blow up and that he could see my knickers just the way he liked. I tried to do handstands and cartwheels, I jumped and twisted, I put on a real display, a proper show – but was it enough that I had performed?

'That was lovely, Sophie,' he said. 'I'd like you to do that again for me sometime – can you wear your blue frilly knickers next time, do you think?'

I smiled broadly. 'Of course I can, Granddad,' I told him, praying my plan had worked.

'You're a really lovely little girl,' he said. 'Now, let me give you a treat – come here.'

I shook my head.

'You'll like it,' he said, reaching out for my hand and pressing it on to his trousers. He unzipped them and this thing popped out: hard and horrible and smelly.

'You'll like it, you'll like it,' he said in that horrible whisper of his.

I knew I wouldn't. It wasn't as big or as black as Dad's but I wanted nothing to do with it. In the back of my mind, I wondered what Mum would say if she saw me touching it. Would she protect me? Would she tell him he was a beast? Or would she just shrug and walk away?

He went on and on, and eventually lost patience.

'Come here and stop being so silly,' he snapped with it still sticking out of his trousers. He rustled the paper bag of sweets. 'Ah, Sophie – be nice to your granddad.'

He pulled me towards him and put my hands on it, just like Dad used to do. I felt sick. I don't even want to write these words as it brings it all back. All I want to say is that he made me move my hands up and down while he breathed strangely, then, after not very long at all, he went to the bathroom. I still didn't know why he did that, but I was glad to see the back of him.

When he returned, I got a handful of sweets.

'Good girl, Sophie,' he winked. 'Good girl.'

It wasn't just him. There were men everywhere. Men leering at Mum, Mum saying things that made me uncomfortable. I looked at men differently now. They seemed much more threatening, because I thought that all of them did the things to little girls that Granddad and my dad did to me.

Mum loved the attention of men and sought it out wherever she could. Any time we went shopping, or went to Grandma's – any time we went anywhere really – she always seemed to need to 'pop' in somewhere. There was a row of shops on the main street near where we lived and, for a while, she had something going on with the butcher that bothered me in a way I couldn't put my finger on. Every time we walked past, he made a strange gesture with his arm that I couldn't understand. He would fold one arm up at the elbow, and put his other hand on the upper arm. I thought it was a rude gesture as some of the boys at school did it, and it made me feel uncomfortable. What made me feel even more uncomfortable was that Mum seemed to like it. She'd laugh and toss her hair as we went past, wiggling her bum as she walked.

Mostly, we'd go in to see the butcher, Daryl, on our way home. She'd tell me to wait outside on the steps with the boys, and I'd hear her giggling with Daryl inside the shop. One day, she said she'd be a while and I saw her disappear up the stairs inside with him. There was another butcher there, a horrible looking bloke with big googly eyes who looked shifty. He curled his finger to me and wriggled his eyebrows, licking his lips as he did so. I knew, I just knew, that he was one of those men, the men who liked to touch little girls. I looked away and kept busy with Mark and Alex.

When Mum came out a bit later she said, 'What's wrong with your face?'

I shook my head, not wanting to say anything.

'Kenny says you're a right stroppy little cow,' she went on, nodding her head to the shifty-looking butcher who had wriggled his finger at me. 'He's only being friendly – you need to learn a few things.'

Every time she went back to see Daryl, Kenny would leer at me. I realized on the second visit that Daryl and Mum were actually in a room above the shop that was directly above where I was sitting on the step. I could hear them having sex and I felt sick. I'm pretty sure everyone in the shop could hear them too as my mum had quite a reputation with men and didn't care what people thought.

I did. I cared.

Granddad was one of the men who made me feel uncomfortable now. He was always touching me, looking inside my knickers and feeling me in private parts. He liked to push my pants to one side and really stare at me. I was just a child, there was nothing to look at, but he did anyway, over and over again.

I did say, 'Don't do that – I don't like you doing that, Granddad,' but he would always answer, 'It's fine Sophie, it's really fine, don't worry.' It was as if I was getting bothered about something that didn't matter, but I knew, in my heart, that it *did* matter. If it didn't matter, I wouldn't feel this bad surely?

He wasn't nasty to me, and he always gave me sweets after he had had a look – as if that was all I needed. He had also started rubbing himself on me and making me touch him every single time I was there, there was never any respite. I could feel his *thing*, a thing just like the one Dad had poking out of his pyjamas. It was hard and horrible as he pushed it up and down on me as he kept me sitting on his lap, facing him. It was pushing into my private parts and felt like it would make me sick. Granddad began breathing heavily just as Dad had done.

'I don't like this – please stop,' I said.

'It's all right, it's fine,' he said, always in quite a gentle voice as if I could be calmed down into liking it.

'But I don't like it, Granddad, I don't want you to do it,' I told him.

'I won't hurt you, I won't hurt you, Sophie,' he said, but he *was* hurting, and he was being rough. Eventually, he'd stop and say, 'You sit next to me,' as he patted the sofa. However, no sooner had I sat down than he would leave the room. I didn't know why that happened, but when he came back he wasn't breathing funnily any more.

That went on for a while. On another occasion, he was playing and tickling me while I was on the floor. He was lying at the side of me, and his hands were wandering. He lifted my skirt up and pushed my knickers to the side, then began to stroke me down there. After a while, he touched my bottom.

'Please stop, Granddad,' I said, 'I don't like it; I've told you I don't like it.'

Just as he was about to say something, just when he was about to tell me it was fine as he always did, my mum walked in. She looked from him to me and back again.

This was what I had always wondered about – what would she do if she found out? I should have known – she walked back out of the room and didn't say a word.

There could have been no doubt about what my granddad was doing to me, and there was no doubt that Mum had seen it. Now, there was no doubt that she didn't care. She had seen an old man abuse me and it didn't even register with her. She couldn't have cared less.

When we got home, she said, 'Was he touching you?'

I nodded – grateful that she had brought it up when I thought she would just ignore it, and desperately hopeful that she would now come to my rescue. I should have known better.

'You let him, I suppose?' she continued. 'Enjoy it, did you? You let him touch you down there, you dirty little bitch. Well, this changes everything. You're a woman now, aren't you?'

I was seven years old.

It did change everything in her eyes.

After she had seen Granddad abuse me, and after she had justified it to herself, the floodgates opened. When each boyfriend departed, I would get a blow by blow account of what they'd done. It was beyond what she had previously said, and it often involved me.

'Oh, he fucked me good and hard, that one,' she'd say, acting all breathless when she closed the door after another 'uncle' had left. 'You know what – I think he liked you too. You could probably make a few bob there.'

I was growing up quickly but I actually had no idea whether she was serious. With every man who came to our house, she would tell me what they had done and, always, always, tell me whether they wanted to have sex with me too, or whether I was too ugly, or whether they preferred her, or whether they had a friend that she could get for me. It was obscene and I was terrified that she would keep her word one day and bring a man home for me.

She walked in on me and Granddad on more than that occasion. She never said anything and I suppose all it did was prove to Granddad that he could do whatever he liked since my own mother didn't care. When we got home, she would always launch into me.

'That's your granddad!' she'd say, as if I didn't know. 'What do you think you're doing?'

She had rewritten the entire situation and I was now a seven-year-old temptress luring my granddad on to the floor of his living room, rather than an abused little girl who had no one to turn to.

I would sometimes say, 'I don't want him to touch me, Mum,' but she just snorted and left the room, saying I was a little 'slut'. She knew it was happening all right, but wasn't prepared to do anything to break up the family, although she was perfectly happy to sacrifice me.

Chapter 9

A little something

This family moved into the area last month . . .
health visitor not available, but appears that there
was some hearsay that there was child abuse. Last
week on Wednesday morning seen by Doctor – he
saw on child's buttocks very deep bruising by mark
of hand. When questioned, Mrs Gilmore denied
hitting the child. Doctor's receptionist said there is
a lot of gossip.
Social work report 4325G/
Sophie Gilmore

I told them I had decided not to take action
over Sophie's injury but to allow her to remain at
home. I told her that I was convening a case
conference to which the Police, the Doctor, the
Health Visitor, the Housing and Social Security
would be invited, as was myself and X (another
member of the team).
Social Services Department report 4325G/
Sophie Gilmore

'Come and get your tea!' Mum shouted to me one night. Mum wasn't an exciting cook – we lived on chips most of the time. When Dad was at home and working, the food was better, but when he was away it was all convenience food that did nothing for us, but at least our bellies were full.

I should have known that was too normal.

Mum still wanted me to commit suicide and was always playing mind games. She was so cruel, really cruel.

She'd been cooking the Sunday meal and my brothers and Dad were all there. I went into the kitchen and looked at what was on my plate.

'You better eat all of that,' she said. 'I've put something special in it for you. A little something for Sophie.'

I had no idea what she was talking about.

'What?' I asked. 'What have you put in it?'

'You'll see!' she laughed.

'Is it something bad, Mum?' I enquired, scared.

'Depends on how you look at it,' she smirked. 'You had better eat it all, Sophie – every last drop. And . . . don't give any of it to your brothers. I don't want them poisoned.'

'You've poisoned it?' I asked, horrified. 'You've put poison in my dinner?'

'Yes, I have,' she smirked. She waited for a moment. 'Or have I?'

I took my plate through to the living room where we always ate. Mum was still in the kitchen so I hid my food under the sofa. I had no idea whether there was anything in it or not; it almost didn't matter, because the very thought of it terrified me.

Obviously, she was going to find it. She cleaned all the time. Every day before we went out, she had rituals. She'd get us all outside and then tell us to wait while she went back into the house to check everything. She would say things, mutter to herself. I don't know what she was saying, but it sounded the same every time before she shut the door and locked it. The house was always clean and tidy, never a mess, and the social workers liked that. They always commented on it in the reports. They seemed to have no idea that a house that looked clean superficially could be rotten to the core.

Even when I was hiding the food, I knew she would find it, but I just needed to buy myself time. Although I wanted to die, both to escape and to make her happy, the thought of putting an unknown quantity of unknown poison into my body willingly was beyond me. She found it later that night and went ballistic.

'Why didn't you eat your dinner, Sophie? Why did you make this mess? Why did you do that?' she asked.

I didn't know what to say; should I tell her that I was scared? Would that make her more angry?

She dragged me out of the room and into the hall.

'Why don't you eat the lovely food I make you, Sophie?'

'I was scared, Mum . . .' I began.

'What were you scared of, you stupid little bastard?'

'The poison – you said you'd put something in it, and I was scared.'

'Poison? What the fuck are you talking about? Poison in your dinner? Are you going fucking mad?' She slapped me and shoved me back into my room, locking the door behind me.

That was the start of that particular method of torture. From that point on, every meal was given to me with a knowing smirk and a whisper that I should enjoy the special thing she had put in. Did she ever put poison into my food? I have no idea. Sometimes I had to eat it because I was starving, and sometimes I was fine – but there were also occasions when I was violently sick. I don't know whether that was all in my head and I'd convinced myself that she was making me ill, or whether it was nerves or as a result of her poisoning me. I never could tell with her.

I hid a lot of the food and that was the start of my eating disorders. When I did get a chance of 'clean' food, at Grandma's or at school, I would gorge myself, but when I was at home I would either hide it or starve. I actually think she probably hadn't tampered with my food at all, because, when I look back, apart from the physical violence, Mum was quite cautious about what she did to me. For all her talk of wanting me dead, she was clearly careful to give me the idea or means to do it myself – the knife, getting me to starve, drinking washing-up liquid . . . all of these were done by me, and if anyone had found out the extent of it, she could have said I had something wrong in my head rather than that I had done it at her insistence. And, to some extent, she would have been right. I was always thinking of ways to hurt myself that might please her. Maybe she did turn me mad for a while even if I was only seven years old.

Once Mum saw that I was eating the food sometimes, she stopped – the torture held no attraction for her unless I was terrified. By the time I was eight, she preferred starving me and often withheld food for days on end. At weekends, I would only eat if I went to Grandma's house.

When I did get clean food, I ate like a vulture. I was quick and I had no manners. It was all about getting something inside me that wasn't going to poison me. I took money from Mum's purse and went to the chip shop; I remember once, at only seven years old, buying two lots of fish and chips and standing in the doorway outside and shoving it all down my throat as fast as I could. I knew I'd get battered for doing it, but the ache in my belly was all I could think of; the consequences were guaranteed, but I was literally starving.

I'd steal food at home if I got a chance. One day when I came home (I was now coming back myself as Mum wasn't collecting me from school), she was in her bedroom. I rushed to the kitchen and opened the fridge. Dad must have been back because there were sausages and bacon. I grabbed a handful of it all and rushed to my room where I stuffed it all down, completely raw, as fast as I could. It didn't matter that it was disgusting and uncooked, it was food. Of course I was ill as a result, but for that moment while I was eating, I didn't care.

I would sneak a few sausages in my pocket to eat on the way to school some days. By the time I'd been there an hour or so, I'd get terrible tummy cramps and spend most of the day in the loo. Teachers weren't very sympathetic and would accuse me of trying to avoid working – sometimes, they would deny me permission to go to the toilet during class, and I would sit there, terrified, in case I couldn't help myself. Occasionally, I just had to run to the toilet despite the fact that they were shouting at me to come back. I'd rather take the punishment than risk the other kids having something else to taunt me about.

I stole from lunchboxes and bags when I was at school. I wasn't a very good thief; I tended to get caught because I would eat things as soon as I'd pinched them. I'd rummage in the lunchboxes on my way back from the toilet and guzzle anything down as if I hadn't eaten for a month. I can't believe that the teachers didn't notice. I was pale and I looked ill. I was so skinny at that point and I'd lost a lot of weight very quickly, but it didn't seem to occur to them that there was a reason for all of this.

In fact, around this time, I was so pale that even Mum got worried and she took me to the doctor. When we got there, the usual GP was on holiday and there was a locum in his place. Dr Welsh listened as Mum told him no more than I was pale and needed a 'tonic'. He said that he would have to examine me to see what was wrong.

I remember Mum saying that was unnecessary, I just needed a tonic, but he was insistent. I couldn't understand why I needed to stand there in my underwear while he checked, or why he lifted up my pants at one point. For a moment, a fear ran through me that he was a man like all the other men, that he just wanted to touch me in that way, but, thankfully, that time I was wrong.

I knew why I was pale, and Mum did too – I think she wanted a bit of attention, but he wasn't going to find anything out by looking up my knickers at my bum or poking about at me.

I was wrong.

Dr Welsh knew exactly what he was doing.

I had no knowledge of it at the time, but it is clear from my files that this man – the first one to notice anything – immediately contacted the authorities about the bruises he found on me, especially those on my buttocks.

A case meeting – the first of many – was called as a result of Dr Welsh's concerns and my family, well known to the authorities already, was put under scrutiny. The report from that time says that there were members of staff from the local authority, a health visitor, a teacher, someone from the housing welfare department, a man from the NSPCC child-abuse special unit, a senior social worker and two police officers present. It states:

The health visitor Miss Thomas advised that a locum doctor saw Sophie at surgery. Mother had brought her to see GP as child was pale. During examination he noticed extensive bruising on the skin in the shape of a hand across the child's buttocks. The mother denied knowledge. Miss Thomas went to family but Sophie at school. Dr Welsh contacted by phone – he confirmed the above but his referral to health visitor was entirely intuitive. Social Services visited three days later – father aware of the bruise and acknowledged he had inflicted it with a slipper as chastisement for Sophie helping herself to some tablets. He advised of his anxiety about this and other aspects of her behaviour. Mother not available nor was Sophie seen. Next day, mother agreed that the bruise was caused by her husband. She complained of Sophie 'throwing food on the floor'. When the discrepancy in their accounts was mentioned they acknowledged that this was probably a different occasion and it was implied that Sophie is regularly physically chastised. Social worker and health visitor were of the opinion that there are problems in the marriage and that these are being taken out on Sophie.

Someone had finally noticed.

The principal social worker in the authority then wrote to Dr Welsh:

It is evident that the bruising was caused by the father. It is not proposed that we take proceedings in the Juvenile Court but [offer] help of various kinds. I would like to take this opportunity to thank you for your initiative, which has brought this family's problems to our notice.

We were on the radar more than we had been, but I was still left at home. The irony was that those bruises were only a few of many, and it was often Mum who left them there. Dad hit me a lot too, but she was worse, because she was with me every single day and she had her campaign of terror against me, which was psychological and emotional as well as physical. I had no escape from her.

I thank God that Dr Welsh was the locum that day – would anything ever had happened if someone else had examined me? Actually, would they have examined me at all? Would they have just accepted my mum's claim that I was off colour and given me some vitamins? I've always wondered why Dr Welsh did dig a little deeper. What was there about us, and about my mum, that made him scratch below the surface? As the reports say he admits that it was largely instinctual, but that's not to be underestimated. Something made him think it wasn't right, and when he had the chance to look at me he found the bruises. No one would have listened to a locum who said that he just 'felt' a family wasn't all it seemed to be, but a doctor making a report that stated he could see hand marks on the bottom of an emaciated child was another matter.

As soon as the authorities starting looking at us in a bit more detail, one thing was obvious to them – I was a child with far too much adult responsibility. I was still bearing the weight of most of the contact with the authorities, and that must surely have been logged somewhere, though I can't find it in the reports. Did they find nothing unusual about a small child making the vast majority of the phone calls, requesting emergency loans – in fact, negotiating everything? Mum usually had an answer for most things, but I can't see how they wouldn't have thought this was an important point. Yes, there are many references made to me taking on too many adult responsibilities, but I can't see why, when there is every single note ever made about planning a visit, missing a visit and rearranging a visit, that there isn't anything logged about the many, many calls I made.

We had always had lots of officials in our lives – social workers, benefit officers, people from the housing department – but they were now coordinating and sending one another the reports they made on us. Half the time, Mum would deliberately be out of the house when she knew they were coming to visit, but that was now being logged too.

There were comments in the files about the boys being well-cared for, but, what no one knew was that by the time I was eight, I was the one looking after them. I loved my brothers so much, despite the fact that they sided with Mum and she tried to turn them against me, getting them to call me names and use the horrible words that she was so fond of against me. I was the one who washed them and made sure they had a bath when she was out with other men or lying in bed. For almost a year, I was the one who raised them, because Dad was hardly ever there and Mum seemed to have one boyfriend after another.

I'd shake Mum awake every morning and remind her that I had to go to school. She'd grunt or swear at me, usually with a strange man at her side. Most of the time I didn't get to school but every morning I hoped I would because there was normality there – and food. Sometimes she'd tell me I wasn't going and that I needed to stay at home with the boys, while she spent the day in her room making strange noises with whatever man had appeared. Sometimes they would both go out drinking, leaving the three of us alone, but there were days when she would say, 'Fine, get them ready and piss off.' On those days, I would take Alex to my grandma's house and then either take Mark with me to school – he was a few years below me – or we would bunk off for the day together.

On some mornings, I would take money from her purse. I knew I'd get hit for that later, but I needed to feed Mark. One day, the boredom and frustration and hunger and anger all came together. We were wandering around town in the rain – a little girl of eight and her much younger brother, who everyone was trying very hard to ignore. We came to the local supermarket and I said to Mark that we should go inside and take shelter for a while, as well as to kill time.

When we got in, for some reason, I grabbed a trolley. We went round all the aisles, filling it as if we were grown-ups doing the weekly grocery shop. It was brilliant! We were so happy as we piled in sweets and crisps and treats. We selected everything that we never got unless we were at Grandma's house, but I also put in the things that I knew 'normal' families needed: milk, bread, cheese, bacon, eggs, sausages, everything that would make good meals. Still no one was watching us. I guess that people can make themselves completely blind to what is going on under their noses if they want to – it was almost as if I could hear them thinking, *Don't get involved, don't make a scene, leave it to someone else.*

Suddenly, I was struck by a wicked thought. What if I just walked out of the supermarket with the trolley full of lovely things?

I knew that stealing was wrong, even though I did plenty of it; but my thefts had been for food and money from Mum for things that I needed to keep me alive. This would be different. I waited for someone to stop me – I waited to stop myself, but it never happened.

Pushing the overflowing trolley somehow or other, Mark and I left the store – and took it home. There was never a hand on our shoulders, there was never a security guard having a word in our ears. We got away with it, and it was the most exhilarating thing I had ever experienced. I couldn't believe we'd done it. I was shocked at myself, but we were both chuffed to bits.

'Look, Mum – look what we've got! We've got all the shopping!' I said once we'd pushed it home. It took us forever, but we had nothing else to do and I was excited about showing her. Mum didn't know whether to be mad or happy – eventually, self-preservation kicked in and she was happy, very happy. She had done nothing wrong as far as she could see it, and she had a trolley full of food for free. It was the first and only time I can ever remember thinking she was pleased with me. I wasn't beaten that night – it was worth it.

I was so desperate for normality, but my life was a million miles away from it. I wanted what everyone else had. I wanted a bag of sweets that didn't come from Granddad. I wanted fifty pence to go to the ice-cream van – once I had even ordered a cone and when it was time to hand the money over, I gave the woman a handful of stones, hoping she'd take pity on me. I wanted a cuddle from a mummy who loved me – I'd never ever get that. I could steal food, but I could never get what I really wanted, I could never get her love.

I was still running away a lot, not just because Mum was telling me to, but because I needed to get away. I was staying off school whenever she said I should, or whenever I was too black and blue to go in, but there were also days when Mum thought I was there that I would bunk off, because I couldn't bear being the thickest, the one without friends and the one who was smelly.

Mum was still tormenting me. She had given up on her claims that she was poisoning my food, but although she was feeding me again, I was still eating whatever I could, whenever I could. As a result, I was getting fat, which was something else to mark me out from the other kids. Mum still hit me a lot, told me I was a useless bastard, a smelly Paki bitch, and would often come up with new ways to 'get' me. One day, when I was standing behind the sofa, she got in front of it and wedged me between it and the wall. She kept shoving until my ribs were being squeezed so hard that I thought I would collapse. She was laughing all the time and saying she was going to kill me.

I'm not sure when I realized that, actually, she wasn't going to murder me. That wouldn't be her style at all, she wanted me to do things to myself; she didn't want to get her hands dirty.

While all the professionals were looking at what was going on at home, none of them could have imagined what was happening with my granddad – although perhaps if someone had asked the right questions, and made me feel safe, I would have told them.

Granddad would fiddle with himself when he looked at me and I could see it getting bigger. I would tell him I didn't like it, but he just whispered, 'It's all right, it's all right.' He smelled of cheese, *it* smelled of cheese. He was always hot down there and when he started to pull his trousers down, the stench of him always hit me. He would put his penis in his own hand and hold it to me as if I should be pleased. When I had to touch it, I felt that I would be sick. The heat was overpowering and just as I thought I couldn't bear it any longer, he would disappear to the toilet. When he came back, he'd breezily say, 'All right, Sophie – want some sweets?' I always felt a bit bewildered – and disgusted with myself that it had happened again.

He would scan me from top to bottom. I think he liked the little-girl look; it was as if he was almost salivating when he looked at me. He paid so much attention to my knickers, my socks – all the 'packaging' that is around a small child; that was what he got off on.

When Grandma and Mum came back from the shops, he was nice as ninepence to them. Grandma could never have known what he had been doing. He'd chat about how the time had flown and we'd barely had time to start playing. Once he laid me down on the dining-room table and lifted my skirt up, took my knickers down and started stroking me down there as he masturbated himself. He couldn't stop touching me. Eventually – I'll admit this, though it's terrible – I gave up telling him to stop. I just knew he would keep doing it and I was wasting my breath so all I wanted was for it to be over. That made me hate myself even more. Everything to do with me was bad. I would imagine I was someone else, living a normal life in a normal family, being loved – that was all I had to take me away. I thought of those good things while he was touching me, and then, before I knew it, he was off, with his trousers round his ankles, away to the bathroom. I ended up just wanting to get it over with on every visit.

One day, he said, 'Come into the bedroom with me, I want to show you something.'

The bedroom he shared with Grandma was lovely – it had signs of her all over. The bedspread and curtains matched with a delicate floral pattern, and her things were everywhere. There was jewellery and make-up and hairbrushes, clothes hanging from the wardrobe doors, the smell of her perfume in the air. It was a horrible contrast – the memories of the grandma I loved and this perverted monster in front of me.

He told me to sit on the bed, then went and took something out of his bedside drawer.

'Look at this!' he said with excitement in his voice.

It was a pack of playing cards. The pictures on them were all of naked women in various poses, legs open in most of them.

'What do you think of that?' he asked. 'Do you like that?'

'No,' I answered unequivocally.

He looked confused.

He showed me another card.

'Don't you think she's got lovely breasts?' he said, pointing at the new card.

'No,' I said.

'Well, what do you think of them?' he pressed. 'Which do you like best?'

'I don't like any of them, Granddad.'

'Well – tell me what you do like, and I'll find a picture.'

He seemed to think it was a matter of finding the right pornographic image, that I was just being choosy – not that I didn't want to look at the cards.

'I like her,' he said, putting one card in my hand. 'Do you? Would you like to touch her? I would,' he told me lecherously.

He kept asking me questions:

What do you think of them?

Do you like that she has her legs open?

See all that hair on her between her legs – do you like that best?

Look at her breasts – they're huge. You'll be like that one day, will you like that? Will you show me?

Go on, Sophie, choose your favourite.

Go on.

Go on.

Go on.

I felt nothing. Finally, after he went on and on, wanting me to feel something, wanting me to be turned on by them and say what I liked, I pointed to one without looking.

'She's best,' I said.

'Do you think?' he replied, sounding disappointed.

'She has a nice smile,' I told him.

'Smile?' he laughed. 'Look at her bottom, look at her breasts, look at what's between her legs – her smile?'

He kept looking at the cards himself as I gazed off to the side, then he started masturbating himself, going between looks at the cards and at me. He then stood up and made for the door to go to the bathroom. Just before he left, he seemed to have a change of heart.

'Come with me, Sophie. Come and have a look,' he suggested.

'I don't want to.'

'Oh, stop being a moan – come here.'

He took me by the hand and led me to the bathroom that was opposite his bedroom. He told me to look at his penis and it seemed yellow. The smell hit me again and I thought I would be sick. The whole sight of him was disgusting. I could even see shit in his pants.

Showing me the cards, getting me to go to the loo and look as he masturbated into the sink became his thing to do. That was his new pattern and it went on for a while.

I was getting older and by the time I was eight what should have been the normal part of my life was erratic too. I was hardly at school. I didn't think I would get into trouble because I didn't think anyone really noticed me – if they did, wouldn't they do something? I would be kept off on Mum's whims, but I was also staying away when it suited me too. There was nothing at school for me. My attempted friendships with Katy and Wendy had been disastrous, and there were no teachers who spared me a kindly word. I spent more time away from school than at it, roaming the streets, looking for safe places I could run to when Mum threw me out, stealing food. What I didn't realize was that truanting would save me – it would take a long time, but it would finally happen.

Chapter 10

Nice, normal, fine

Sophie has gone through a difficult period since
the last report. Her relationship with her family
continues to have highs and lows. In school,
Sophie presents a few problems – she puts very
little effort into basic subjects.

Social work files 4325G/

Sophie Gilmore

I was still spending a lot of time at my grandparents'
house. Granddad wasn't working much and Grandma had
gone part-time at the florist where she had been based for
some years. I often went for sleepovers, which I hated
since I realized that having Grandma in the house wouldn't
actually stop him from touching me if he thought she was
asleep. She always had a glass of sherry before bed while
they watched TV, and I noticed that he was careful to top
it up a few times when I was there to make her sleep even
more soundly. The fact that she snored very loudly was
even more helpful to him because it meant that he could
always listen out for any sign that she was awake.

It was common for him to come into the spare room where I slept, even if Mark or Alex were there too, and to start fiddling about with me under the covers. He had no shame, and it seemed as if it was all he ever thought about. He would come into the room when I was dressing or undressing, under the excuse of 'helping' me to get ready, and even when I said I didn't need any help, he'd loudly say to Grandma that I was getting a big girl now but that I could still use a helping hand from my own granddad. It was the last thing I wanted.

By this point, to my shame, I'd almost given up. He was always looking at me and touching me, and he was obsessed with me touching him *there* until just before he ejaculated, at which point he would run off to the bathroom and (I know now) finish himself off. It was never-ending. I got no pleasure from it, how could I? But he was constantly telling me that it was all fine, all nice, all something that was good.

One night when I sleeping over, I heard Granddad say to Grandma after dinner, 'I think I'll take Sophie out for a little drive.'

'Oh, she'll like that,' said Grandma. 'What a treat, Sophie — just you and your granddad! Ah, you dote on that girl, Arthur, you really do.'

It was no treat for me and I didn't think for a moment that he wouldn't have something planned. He drove us around town for a while and got me a bag of chips. That calmed me down a bit, because he usually only gave me something to eat *after* he'd abused me, so the fact that I was getting fed now seemed like a good omen. He chatted a little and seemed fine, the sort of Granddad I liked him being, but then when we hadn't been out for long he said we should start heading back. It seemed quick, but I said nothing. He went a different way and, for some reason, pulled into a car park at the local woods. It was the sort of place with trails and picnic areas, but I couldn't see why we would be here at this time of night. It wasn't dark, but it was getting there.

'Come on,' he said, 'let's have a little walk.'

I saw no problem with that even if it was odd, so I followed him. He didn't take one of the recognized trails, instead he took a path that didn't seem very well worn but which went right into the trees.

I was walking behind him, and after we'd been going a little while he turned round to me and said, 'Here we are!'

I should have known.

His penis was hanging out of his trousers and he had a big smile on his face.

'Isn't this nice?' he said, and I wasn't even sure whether the deluded old pervert meant the setting or what he wanted me to do. I know that he would have loved it if I had said I enjoyed it all too, but that was a step too far. I could bear it, I could bear anything, but I would not pretend that it was my choice.

'Come on then, Sophie,' he said, licking his lips. 'Touch it – go on, it's fine, it's fine.' The horrible whispering voice that I hated so much was there again and he raised his eyebrows to me, encouraging me to come closer and take it in my hand. I did. I wanted it all over as quickly as possible, but, once I had done what he wanted, got him to where he wanted to be, there was no bathroom for him to run to, so I stood there as he finished the job himself. I've no idea why he always did that; given what else he was doing to me, I would have thought that he would have preferred for me to do the entire filthy business, but I don't know what was going on in his mind.

That was the start of our drives. Drives to isolated parts of the woods where he would get me to touch him and he'd touch me, just as casually as if we were in his own living room. Every time we got back, Grandma would act as if he was the nicest Granddad in the world, and I'd hate the way he duped her just as much as I hated what he did to me.

'Did you have a nice drive?' she'd ask.

'Lovely,' he'd reply, leering at me behind her back. 'Lovely – wasn't it, Sophie? We had a great time – must do it again soon, don't you think?'

I'd stomp off to my bedroom and would often hear comments from Grandma that hurt me so much.

'Oooh, she's getting a bit moody, isn't she, our Sophie?'

'It's just her age, Grace,' Granddad would say. 'Cut her some slack, it's just her age.'

'You indulge that girl, Arthur,' Grandma would say, and they'd settle down on the sofa together for the evening, while I waited in my room to see if he would visit me again that night.

He'd stopped pretending we were playing. It was all very open now with him – he knew what he wanted and he knew he wanted me to give him it. I suppose it was only a matter of time before it escalated, but there was no preamble.

Once day, while he was standing at the window of the new flat he shared with Grandma, watching her and my mum walk down the street and go round the corner to the shops, he said, 'Here, Sophie – lick this.'

He'd taken his penis out but I couldn't quite process what he was asking me to do.

Lick it? *Lick* that disgusting, cheese-stinking, bulging monstrosity? Why on earth would I do that?

I laughed.

'Don't be daft,' I told him.

'What are you talking about?' he said. 'Go on – it's fine, it is, it's fine. Lick it. Kiss it. Put it in your mouth.'

THAT?

Put THAT in my mouth?

I thought he must be mad and I had no idea why he thought I would want to do what he was asking – he couldn't pretend it would be 'fun' surely?

'Sophie,' he said to me, 'it'll be fine, it really will.'

I knew by this time that there was no getting out of any this, no one was going to save me and no one would believe me if I told them. After all, my own mother knew what was going on and she didn't care, preferring instead to blame me as if I had engineered it all. As I thought of all this, I realized I would have to do this, just as I would have to do anything he wanted. So, I did. I put it in my mouth and I followed his directions. I thought I would be sick, but, every time I gagged, he told me again, 'It'll be fine,' and I knew that if I pulled away, he would make me start all over again. It was better to get it all over and done with – and to not think about the fact that, if I did this, he'd want it again and again. I actually have no idea how I did manage it in the end. I held everything inside myself because I thought I couldn't stop anything.

He was always whispering, it drove me nuts, the way his conniving voice and shifty eyes always seemed to be there.

'It won't take long, Sophie – just get down on your knees.'

I felt the pressure of his hand, pushing me down, telling me I had to do it – but he was still being 'nice', he was never nasty at all. He was trying to be a good granddad I think, and he thought he was. He got hold of my head and positioned me. He kept moving my head about until I was almost fastened there. I was gagging but he didn't stop; he kept moving my head and moving his hips. I thought he'd choke me to death, the dirty bastard.

I tasted something horrible, then he was off. I was left on my knees while he went to the bathroom

I felt so disgusting.

I could taste him, I could smell him – in my nose, in my face, everywhere.

Dirty, dirty bastard.

I wished he had choked me; I wished I was dead.

From that day on, he kept doing that every opportunity he got – he'd found something new. Every time I was there, he wanted oral sex. When Mum and Grandma went out, he wanted it. When I was staying over, he wanted it. When he took me to the woods, he wanted it. It stays with me to this day – whenever I do that with a man, that's the memory I have, no matter if there's a smile painted on my face.

I became immune to it and just wanted it over and done with each time. I know that's a common reaction amongst abused kids – you know what's going to happen, so you want it to finish – but it still makes me feel awful that I let him do those things. I hate him for what he did to me.

I would have daydreams about what would happen if he did choke me and Grandma came back and found my dead body on her living-room floor. In my mind he was always still standing there with his horrible stinking penis hanging out as Grandma screamed at the loss of me and what he'd done. I almost wanted that to happen, but I still didn't tell the police or the social workers, I held back from telling anyone anything that might result in him being punished for what he was doing to me.

Something happened at that point in my life. From then to the present day, that's how I think of myself – as something to give sex. If I get sex right, then I can convince myself that everything else will fall into place. I pride myself on pleasing men, giving good oral, everything. I was always proud of that. Even if I can get nothing else right in a relationship, I can do that. When I've been with men and they say how good I am at giving oral sex, I'm pleased because that's the only value I think I have, but I also want to scream at them – and how the FUCK do you think I learned? While you're lying there enjoying it, I'm remembering how it all started and how I got so good. I might look happy, I might look as if I'm enjoying myself too, but I'm dying inside, remembering every time he made me do that.

He was still obsessed with my knickers. I had a pair of light blue ones with lace and he got very excited when he saw them.

'Wear them next time,' he said to me when I left that day. 'Wear them for your granddad.'

I put them in the bin that night, sick at the thought that

he believed I would want to please him in such a perverted way.

I don't know whether things were ramping up with Granddad because I was getting older, or because I was getting bigger – I could take more I suppose, or perhaps it was because he could see that I wouldn't tell anyone and Mum didn't care enough to stop it.

One day, after he'd started making me give him oral sex, we were in his bedroom and he had those naked cards out again. I could never understand why he was so fixated on them. In fact, even now, I'm not sure why. He must have had pornographic magazines, men like him always do, but it was those cards he showed me, over and over, always trying to get me to have a conversation with him about the women as if we were chatting about the weather. I wondered if he wanted me to pose like them or if he wanted me to get sexually excited about them too, though that was never going to happen. That day I was expecting him to just show me them and get me to masturbate him as usual, but he told me to lie down on the bed and spread my legs.

At first, I thought my suspicions had been right – he wanted me to copy the women in the cards, but then he took his trousers and pants off and lay beside me. I wasn't stupid enough to think he was going to sleep, and it wasn't long before he started touching me. Then, to my horror, he tried to get on top of me. I was so small that there was no way he could actually lie on me, but he sort of held himself up on his elbows and tried to force himself into my body. I didn't care who heard me – as soon as he touched me there, I started screaming. Mum had told me plenty about sex and there was no way I was going to let him do that to me, not without a fight.

He got off me immediately and started whispering, 'No, no, it's fine. Don't worry, Sophie, it's fine – we won't do that, not just now. No, it's fine, it's fine.'

He pulled his trousers back on and I ran downstairs. Granddad gave me plenty of sweets that day and he didn't touch me again on that visit. For a little while, he seemed to be working more. He still worked on the railways and I always loved the visits to Grandma's house when he wasn't there; I hated him by this stage.

He tried on plenty of other occasions to rape me, and, each time, got a little further, a little closer to his goal. Whenever he did go inside me a bit, it was agony. If I slept over, he would try it. Every time he did something, he wanted to know if it was nice. I think he wanted me to act as if I was a willing partner, that I was well on my way to becoming a woman and he was making me happy. It couldn't have been further from the truth. I screamed every time – but I have no idea how much he would have kept pushing for it to happen if there hadn't been another development in my life.

There are so many things that hang over me from my childhood, but what really appals me is that I could have, and should have, been taken away since the people who were looking at my situation could see that there was plenty wrong with it. I now know that the bruises that had been discovered on me by the GP had resulted in a lot of discussion and many reports. It would seem that my parents had been questioned a lot, but that they never stuck to the same story, which was causing concern. Another file that repeats some earlier material says:

> On further questioning, Mrs Gilmore admitted that the bruises were not caused by the child falling over but rather by Mr Gilmore hitting the child. I asked her why Mr Gilmore hit the child and she said it was because the child had been spitting. I put it to her that Mr Gilmore said the child had stolen ointment. She said this was another occasion he hit the child. Mrs Gilmore said that after Mr Gilmore had hit the child she asked him to stop but he did not and he hit the child a number of times. I asked Mrs Gilmore if she thought that Mr Gilmore's temper was uncontrollable and she said that she thought it was, but that he had now had a fright and he would not hit Sophie so hard again. I asked her how she knew this. She replied that she knew he definitely wouldn't. I asked her again how she could know and she said she couldn't explain but she definitely knew. Beyond the fact that he had a scare there seemed no other apparent reason why he would not hit Sophie again.

They were lying – and the only way Mum could know that no more bruises would show was if she stopped inflicting them. Yes, Dad did hit me, and he had caused the mark that the GP had reported, but Mum had done much worse, much more often.

Now that so many people were watching us in an official capacity, Mum's warnings had actually come true. We were under the microscope and she wasn't about to let the blame fall on her.

'Your father is a very violent man, Sophie,' she had started saying to me and I, like the dutiful daughter I was, didn't point out that he wasn't the only one in that house with those tendencies.

She was always dropping little hints, little suggestions:

If anyone asks if he hits you, it's fine to say he does.

If you want to tell people how violent he is, that's fine.

Your father's to blame for everything wrong with this family — people should know that.

I got the message. Dad was to carry the can for everything, and she was to escape scot-free. Despite everything, I loved my mum and I wanted her to love me. From that point on, though I was still wary of telling officials anything, when I did have to talk I'd speak about Dad's violence. I never told about Mum, never, and yet she was getting worse. The boundaries were completely blurred by the time I was eight. One night, when Dad was gone and the boys were asleep, she came into my room all dolled up.

'Come on, Sophie,' she said, shaking me awake. 'We need to get going.'

'Where?' I asked. 'What's wrong?'

'Nothing's wrong — we're going out.' She seemed excited and oddly happy. 'Get dressed — make sure you look nice. In fact, wear your blue dress and then come through and I'll put some make-up on you.'

I did as I was told, but did think it odd that we were going out at night. We ended up walking into what I knew was a really rough area.

'Is it safe here, Mum?' I asked.

'Course it is,' she replied. 'It's full of coppers watching

the prostitutes!' she laughed. When she saw I didn't understand, she said, 'It's the red-light district, Sophie. God, do you know nothing? It's as safe as anywhere.'

Mum was wearing a really short skirt and lots of lipstick, but we didn't seem to be going anywhere. She walked off as quickly as her high heels would allow and I followed her to an all-night cafe. We got two cups of tea and she went to the jukebox to put on her favourite tune, 'It Started with a Kiss' by Hot Chocolate. She put it on over and over again. We were there for ages and not one person asked why she was out after midnight with an eight-year-old child painted up to look like a mini-prostitute.

There was a taxi rank across the road from the cafe.

'Go and talk to him,' she said at one point, indicating a cab driver who was standing outside his taxi.

'I don't want to,' I said. 'What would I say?'

'Ask him if he wants to come home with me,' she whispered. 'Go on. Show him who I am then he'll come.'

That was another pattern she started that night. Most of the time she'd choose who I was to ask (it was always Asian men), but sometimes, as if it were a treat for me, she'd say I could pick whichever man I wanted. I preferred it when she didn't do that.

A few men would say, 'Why's she asking you to get a taxi for her?' Then I'd have to explain that we weren't hiring them for a lift back to the house; no, my mother was sending her child out to pimp for her. She had told me to inform them that I was to say they could have sex, so I said just that.

'Would you like my mum to give you some sex?' I said

awkwardly. Some of them laughed and told me to get myself home, but some of them couldn't believe their luck.

'What did you say?' they'd ask.

'Would you like my mum to give you some sex?' I'd repeat.

'Is this a joke?' some would reply.

'No – would you like some sex from her?' I'd ask bold as brass. We'd get into the taxi and she'd be in the front with whatever man she'd got that night.

When we got in, she'd be nice to them, as if they had been invited round for anything other than the obvious.

'Sophie, show us your manners and make a cup of tea for . . .?' She never knew their names, and I suspect they gave her fake ones anyway. I'd go off to make hot drinks and, by the time I got back, they'd be up to all sorts. I was glad when she was too busy to pay any attention to me, glad when I knew she was busy having sex with strangers, because I could check on Mark and Alex, then go to my room.

I was disgusted by her behaviour but it went on every single night for about six weeks. I couldn't go to school then because I was exhausted. It seemed like another compulsion for her, those nights at the taxi rank with the drivers, then it stopped as quickly as it had started.

Some mornings, when the men had gone, she'd say to me over breakfast, 'He was desperate for you, you know. He thought his luck was in when you went over to him offering all sorts. He liked me best, of course, but he would have had you too.'

What was she thinking of? Was I supposed to be

pleased? Flattered? Even in the middle of it all, though, I noticed that she was still keen to emphasize to me that she was better than I was, that the taxi driver liked her more – as if I cared in the slightest. I think she wanted me to be like her – for all I know, she could have been offering me to them, and perhaps that's why she took me with her in the first place. After all, she'd wanted me to open my legs for a fiver from a stranger not so long ago. I do think that if I had said I wanted to have sex with those taxi drivers, she'd have been all for it. She wouldn't have seen me as her daughter, she'd have seen us as two best friends going out on the pull together.

The social workers never knew any of that. I wouldn't have known what to say and I would have felt ashamed that I was part of it anyway. Surely if I was a good little girl, I would have played no part in it? The fact that I was colluding with my mother made me, in my own eyes, as bad as her. So, nothing was said, and everything was instead focussed on the fact that Dad hit me. But there was so much more going on.

Chapter 11

At last

The above-mentioned girl was admitted to
the assessment centre having been made subject
to an Interim Care Order for irregular school
attendance. It is respectfully recommended that
a care order be made in order that appropriate
plans may be made to ensure that she develops
emotionally and a regular pattern of school
attendance can be maintained.
Department of Social Service
report to Juvenile Court
4325G/Sophie Gilmore

I had developed a habit of scanning places, looking out
for safe boltholes, always logging them in my mind in case
I needed them. On one trip into town, I had noticed a
scrap yard that was full of old cars and a thought passed
through my mind that someone could hide there if they
needed to – someone like me.

Mum never really bothered where I was at any time

of the day or night and, like many times before, I'd just had enough one evening. I went to my room early and got locked in as usual, but I knew that it was going to be one of the nights when I would leave, either by sneaking out when Mum's back was turned or escaping when she was busy cleaning. This was turning into a regular occurrence, however I was always concerned about where I would spend the nights when I ran off. It came to me that the scrap-metal yard with all the cars piled up would be perfect. I could climb into one of those and sleep.

So, I left. I didn't bother to close the door quietly, I never did. I suppose I always hoped Mum would come out when she heard me and say that she didn't want me to wander off. I wanted her to say that she was worried about me and that she hated the idea of her little girl being out in the dark, God knows where, all alone. Fat chance. I'd already been picked up by the police twice that month after sleeping rough on park benches, so it looked as if, not only did she not care about me, but she also thought she could run rings round the Social Services as the police must surely have been reporting all this back to them.

I got to the scrap yard and instantly felt as if I'd made the wrong decision. It was a much colder night than I had realized, and I only had on a thin dress that Grandma had given me for my birthday. Still, I had made my choice and I wasn't going back to that hellhole.

There were some cars piled up on top of each other, but there were also some in a row, parked nose to nose. They were all unlocked; they were worthless, I suppose, which seemed apt given how I felt about myself. I chose a nondescript red one, drawn to the colour, which I had always liked. I climbed in and settled myself in the back seat. After a little while – I didn't have a watch but it didn't seem as if much time had passed – I heard someone moving around outside, walking up and down. I wondered if it was a security guard and if he would look in all the cars. If he did, and if he found me, what would he do?

Once I knew he had walked past, I peeked out of the window to see. It wasn't a security guard, it was a homeless man, looking for somewhere to sleep too. I was terrified. I prayed and prayed that he wouldn't choose my car and I tried to work out if I could get out the other side and run fast enough away from him to save myself if I needed to.

For once, my prayers were answered and I heard him get in the car behind me.

Finally, I fell asleep and woke up just as it was starting to get light. As soon as I woke, I recognized a familiar smell in the car and a feeling of dampness on my body. I had wet myself during the night and was now stinking, freezing and starving. I was so wet that I thought I must have actually peed quite a few times, probably through a combination of fear and anxiety.

I wasn't sure what to do. I did want to go home now, but hoped that Mum wouldn't be there. If she was there, I wanted to go somewhere safe, away from her. I walked to the local police station, wet and smelly, and told them I'd run away.

They took my name and address, and there was a

look of recognition on the officer's face when I gave him the details. I knew that Mum would be furious if I came home with the coppers, but I was pretty sure that turning myself in and admitting to having run away for the third time that month would mean that they would have to do something. After all, I had already slept in the park one night until it got too cold and I was forced to go home, as well as wandering about all day in the town centre in the pouring rain and freezing weather. On both occasions the police had found me, and on both occasions they had returned me to Mum, despite me pleading with them to do something, anything, other than that.

I should have known that this time would be no different.

All they did do was take me back home where my mum did her usual act of pretending she was worried while they were there, then beating holy shit out of me once they'd gone.

I was constantly running away. I wanted to be somewhere that Mum couldn't get to me as I was so sick and tired of the beatings, but, mostly, I wanted to be a long distance from Granddad.

The other thing I had started to do regularly was to expose myself in public places. All I knew was sex. It was in every area of my life and my body had, pretty much, been public property for years now. I would take my clothes off when I was hiding at night – sometimes I wanted someone to catch me, other times it was what I dreaded. I would lie naked on slides, in play parks, in cars, on benches – if anyone did see me, they never said a word. I suppose I was attention-seeking, but I wonder whether there was also a need to be in charge of my own body, to be the one who was deciding what to do with it instead of others deciding for me.

Everything was getting worse. It was rare that Dad would be at home, but there was one time when he was there for a few months and it was awful. He was hitting me and Mum. One night, he actually had a knife at my back and said he was going to kill me. Mum was arguing with him and I was screaming my head off. I guess she didn't want him to kill me because that would have spoiled her torture of me, and maybe meant the boys would be taken away.

Eventually, he gave up and walked away with the knife, but I was still scared. I wanted him out of the house – so I told her. I told Mum.

'He's been touching me,' I said. I wanted him to get into trouble.

It was the truth, though he had stopped a long time ago. However, I'd learned to be manipulative and it suited me to tell her now.

I swear her eyes lit up.

'Oh – has he? Has he now? Well,' she said, 'I think we might just have to tell the police, don't you?'

She did. She called the police.

I knew that she hoped if he was found guilty he would be thrown out of the house, but he denied it, of course. He was waiting for me when I got back from the police station and got me on my own as soon as Mum went to put the boys to bed.

'You're lying! You're lying! You're lying!' he shouted.

He threatened me, saying he would kill me for real this time if I didn't retract, so I did. I was given a stern talking to by the police for wasting their time, and Mum battered me from one end of the house to another. I was thrown around like a rag doll.

That was my experience of telling the truth; I had told to get him out and away from us but it hadn't worked.

We were still the family from hell, but we had moved again – this time to an even rougher estate where everyone was harder than us, so I didn't dare continue with my habit of annoying the neighbours. I think I had started it to try to get some attention – if I was really naughty, maybe someone would take me away? That never worked, just as the police never took me somewhere safe when they found me each time I absconded. The last time I had properly caused trouble to the neighbours was one night when I heard non-stop banging coming through the walls. It went on and on, getting into my head. In a fit of annoyance, I shouted, 'Your mum's a prostitute!' It all went quiet; I'd probably hit the nail on the head.

At least it worked, I thought, heading off to bed.

That night, all our windows were smashed.

Mum, Mark, Alex, whatever boyfriend was staying and I were all terrified. People rushed in, looting what little we had, taking everything, including the red boots I loved. I bawled my eyes out for those boots. The police weren't even called, there was no point – our stuff was pretty much worthless, and the estate was largely left to police itself.

What I didn't know was that lots of people were watching other parts of my life and they were finally going to act. It amazes me that it took so long and that it was, eventually, truancy that made them take action.

I had been running away.

I had been getting beaten by Mum since I could remember.

I had been sexually abused by my father

I had been sexually abused by my grandfather.

I had been neglected and unloved.

I had been left to lie in soiled bedding, locked in my room and forced to use a bucket as a toilet.

I had been starved.

I had been mentally tortured and told I was being poisoned.

I had been hit so hard that visible marks were left on me.

I had been told to kill myself

I had been dragged out of bed in the middle of the night to find men for my mother.

I had seen my mother having sex.

And so much more, so much more.

All along, all I'd needed to do to was stay off school.

How simple – if only I'd known I'd have kept away from the first day I was registered and maybe I could have avoided years of this horror.

As it was, the truancy gave the Social Services a kick up the backside as there were legal requirements stating that a child needed to attend full-time education, and that simply wasn't happening with me.

The report that states that momentous decision says with remarkable brevity:

Sophie was made subject of a Care Order in court today.
Mrs Gilmore was annoyed.

I bet she was. The facade she had so carefully constructed for years was finally showing signs of weakness.

There had been a build up. There had been lots of discussions, and Mum did know about them. They always wrote to say when they were coming and they always wrote after that to say they had been and she wasn't there. The social workers were trying to tell Mum that it had gone too far, that I had been off school so much that action had to be taken. She reacted furiously to this, shouting and bawling about discrimination, about being picked on, about poor folk having no rights. She screamed that she was my mother and that she would look after me, while I wondered how she could have the brass neck to lie so much. This went on for a while, but she kept saying they couldn't have me. The irony was that she hated me and had been trying to get rid of me for years, but that was on her terms, whereas this was being forced on her. The authorities finally figured out how she functioned and changed tack. Instead of emphasizing that she had been a bad mother by allowing me to miss so much school, they suggested that she could have a little break if I went into care. They implied that, because of my missed schooling, they could take me to an assessment centre and see how far behind I was. This would take a few weeks, allowing Mum a chance to recharge her batteries without having a truanting child to look after.

Dad had been all for it the whole time, but he had no

idea of the extent of her cruelty towards me. He was no angel, but he had never mentally tortured me the way she had. She backed down when she was offered a get-out, whereas he was just relieved to be ridding himself of the child who was such a problem. He saw me getting up to all sorts and had no idea why I was like that, or so he said – he wouldn't have had to think very hard to remember some of the things he had done in the past – and he claimed that this was a chance to get me 'sorted out'.

So, finally, Mum must have realized that I was going to be taken, and that she could either let it happen against her will or she could save face. She went for the latter option, as anyone who knew her would always have predicted. I had spent a long time desperate for freedom. I had dreamed of being part of another family, being some-one else's daughter, having a mummy who loved me, and I had always hoped someone would notice how bad things were and intervene. It's quite odd, therefore, that I don't really remember much about the actual process of being taken from home to the assessment centre. I know that two people came for me, a man and a woman, and that I went with them in a black car after they had helped me pack my few belongings in a bag.

I don't recall saying goodbye to Mark and Alex, yet I would have felt in two minds about leaving them. I wanted to protect them, but I needed to protect myself more. If I had given in, I would never be able to do anything for them. Also, to be honest, they had been turning on me more and more. They weren't the loving baby brothers of the early days, as Mum had twisted them into hating me too. When she wasn't there, it was better, but if she was around, all three ganged up against me.

So, I knew that I needed to go, and I knew that Mark and Alex were not being treated by her in the same way she treated me, but I do wonder whether the reason I can't recall much of that day is that I've chosen to block it out. Yet again, I had hopes; I dreamed that Mum would rush after me and clasp me to her, weeping that she couldn't live without me. That never happened.

When we got the assessment centre, I was weighed and the nurse said, 'You're a skinny little thing, aren't you?'

I was. My weight went up and down depending on whether Mum was torturing me with food, or whether she was even feeding me at all. Other factors, such as whether I was able to steal food mattered too, but as I'd been away from school for ages, I hadn't been in a position to pinch snacks and lunches from my fellow pupils. I was at a thin stage when I was taken in, but the nurse was kindly, as everyone was, and assured me that 'We'll soon put some meat on your bones.'

I had been apprehensive when I was taken to the assessment centre, but, after the nurse was finished with me and I'd met some more members of staff, the real test came. I had to mix with other children, who were all there for behavioural problems or delinquency. I had no idea how I would do that; I wasn't a child who had been socialized, and I'd never really had friends. All I knew was how to manipulate and lie, how to wreck things and hide my true feelings. I didn't see any reason to change just because I was in different surroundings; in fact, I doubt I could have changed even if I had wanted to.

I was taken into a sort of common room where there were about a dozen children of roughly my age, some a little younger, some a little older. They were all playing and chatting, but when the door opened and I was taken in, it went deathly silent.

'This is Sophie,' said the woman who was in charge of me for that part of the day. 'Let's all make her welcome, shall we?'

A few kids smiled, and I smiled back, but I was weighing them all up. I always weighed everything up: people and surroundings. I couldn't see who the ringleader was, or whether there was someone I needed to watch out for, so, as soon as I was left alone with them, I made it quite clear that I wouldn't be bossed around. I was assertive and loud, and it worked. No one messed with me while I was there, but I didn't really make any good friends either. Lots of reports say the same thing – I manipulated others and acted stroppy. Even when it was obvious that this wasn't an approach that would make me popular, I didn't alter it. I couldn't really, it was all I knew.

As soon as I got to the assessment centre, I started looking for a mother figure. I'd never had the right kind before, and I was terrified that I would be sent back to Mum, but I hoped that if I found one here not only would I get a bit of love, I'd also have more chance of staying. I latched on to every woman I could, in turn. They were all really nice, but they were professional and wise to kids like me. I guess they were fully aware that there were so many lost children there who were all looking for a fantasy mother figure, and they couldn't afford to show favouritism. I took this badly. I took it as more rejection. *Why* didn't they like me more than the other kids? *Why* didn't they like me best? What was it about me that stopped these women adoring me, wrapping me up in cuddles twenty-four hours a day and saying they'd take me away from it all? I wanted a miracle, I wanted what they couldn't give me and I got furious when they wouldn't do what I was after.

I bet they'd seen every trick in the book, but I still tried. I would say I'd hurt myself or I would say someone else had hurt me. I would be noisy and disruptive and violent to get attention, then I'd cry my heart out. I would hide, I would ask for things when they were busy with others, I would compliment them all the time. I would ask them if they liked me a lot, if they thought I was pretty, if they thought I could stay there forever. I was constantly, constantly, constantly at them – and it was always the women, because I thought if I looked hard enough I'd find one who could be my new mummy.

When they didn't all line up for the job, I didn't tell myself it was because of boundaries, because boundaries were something I had no concept of. I told myself they were cold or miserable, or that I was so horrible that no one could love me anyway. My files state many times that I was always looking for a mother figure, and that it was something else that made me unpopular with the other children. I'm not surprised. I took attention away from them, and I guess they were all just as desperate for it as I was.

There was a school in the grounds of the assessment

centre and I started there the morning after I arrived. I was tested in every subject and it was found that I was performing at the level of a child three or four years younger than me. Nothing much was really said about that, the teachers just tried over the next three weeks of my assessment to gently introduce me to ideas and concepts that should have already been obvious to me. It didn't feel like 'normal' school. The teachers were kind and everyone was given time to do their best. Food was clearly never an issue, so I didn't have to sneak out of class to thieve from schoolbags. I was still wetting the bed, but, rather than be cross, staff supported me and understood that it was happening because of stress and a likely medical problem.

What mattered most was that the people looking after me while I was there were well aware that I had, in effect, learning difficulties. I don't mean that in the sense that it is often used for children who have been born with such difficulties; I actually had trouble *learning*. I had missed so much school because of Mum's violence and neglect; I could do basic things: I could write and read and count for instance – just not very well, and not to a level that was appropriate for my age. What I could do, and what was shown on every report and every file, was liaise with adults. I was way beyond my years in that and that is the part I remember most from my stay – no matter what I was being taught or questioned about, I was constantly searching for someone would could save me.

I was also being assessed by psychiatrists who noted:

The above girl was referred for psychiatric examination following irregular school attendance. She presents as a most precocious little girl who feels that her admission to care is entirely her father's fault.

When I had to blame someone, I blamed Dad. It was easier. I could do without him if I had to choose, plus Mum had always warned me that, if asked, I should pin the blame on him. So I did.

There were so many parts of my time at the assessment centre that I enjoyed, even if I was precocious, even if I did lie and manipulate. But it had to come to an end, and all too soon.

When the three weeks were up, Mum came to visit me. I'd been counting the days, not with happy anticipation but with dread. I had been calm and safe for the first time in my life. While my records say that I was wilful and manipulative (and I was), the staff at the assessment centre had no idea just how good it felt for me to be there or how much better behaved I was than in 'real' life.

I had breakfast, as normal, then went back to my room. My stomach was churning and I hadn't really been able to eat anything. Everyone on the staff was nice to me as always, telling me that my mum was coming soon, but actually, all I wanted to hear from them was that she *wasn't* coming, she had been delayed or had decided I could stay there forever. As I waited I thought that every footstep was her. Finally, there was a knock on my door – that could only have been someone from the centre, Mum would never have shown me that courtesy – and there she was.

Would there be a happy reconciliation? Would there hell.

As the social worker stood there, Mum looked at me and all she said was, 'You've got a bottom.'

'What?' I asked, not surprised that she hadn't hugged or kissed me, but wondering what on earth she was talking about. 'What do you mean?'

'You've got a bottom. You're getting fat,' she told me, sitting down on the bed and looking round.

'Sophie's been doing really well,' said the social worker, trying to salvage something from the situation. 'She's eating her meals, going through educational assessment, mixing with everyone.'

'Right,' said Mum as if she couldn't have had any less interest in me and what had been going on in my life.

The social worker seemed to be finding it all a bit awkward. No one said anything for a while, then, cheerily, she said, 'Well, shall I leave you two alone for a bit?' Without waiting for an answer, she left us. It was silent for perhaps five minutes, before Mum told me, 'Get your things.'

'What things?' I asked.

'For fuck's sake. *Your* things, get *your* things,' she replied.

'Why?' I asked, already fearing the answer.

'We're fucking off out of here,' she announced, standing up and opening the door. I did as she told me – old habits die hard – and followed her downstairs to the front door.

'Just popping out for a bit,' she said breezily to the woman on reception. 'Back soon!'

And that was that.

She took me home – and they let her.

I'd had three weeks of bliss – well, bliss compared to what my life was usually like – and Mum simply walked in and stopped it. She didn't want me for me; she hadn't missed me, she'd just decided that her part of the deal had been completed. The three weeks were up and it was time for me to go home.

There must have been phone calls or visits, surely there would have been meetings, but my bulging files are strangely empty of anything referring to this part of my story. There's nothing there. Nothing to say whether Mum was told to bring me back, nothing to say if she got into trouble, nothing to say if an inter-agency emergency meeting was called. There's just a big gap where that part of the story should be.

While the authorities did whatever they did, my life went back to normal. Mum took me home to where Dad and my brothers were waiting. She told me to 'piss off' to my room and ignored me for the rest of the day. I didn't get lunch or dinner or supper. I was locked in just as it got dark, and I wet myself that night as usual.

The next morning, she woke me by whacking my head when she smelled the stinking sheets.

'Oh for Christ's FUCKING sake!' she bawled. 'Did they teach you NOTHING? I thought they'd have you sorted, I thought they might have beaten your filthy ways out of you, but, no, they take you away for three fucking weeks and send you back exactly the fucking same!'

As I listened to the usual taunts of me being a 'dirty little bitch', a 'stinking Paki who should be living in a fucking field', Mum got all her frustrations of the past three weeks out on my little body. Every punch, every slap,

186

every kick was, I felt, a punch, slap and kick at the authorities who had dared to take me away. They had shamed her and she would make them pay, through me.

Mum made it quite clear, as always, that I was *her* child, and she alone would decide what should be done with me.

Chapter 12

In charge

The health visitor reported that when she saw
Mrs Gilmore she received a tirade of abuse. I
explained that I have had numerous dealings with
the Gilmores in the past and felt that there was
little likelyhood [sic] of Sophie being in any danger
from her mother. I felt it much more likely that
Sophie and her mother were working in concert to
manipulate the situation.
Social work files 4325G/

Sophie Gilmore

Mum made it very clear who was in charge the next day.

'Get your fat arse out of bed,' she shouted. 'We're going to my mum's.'

My heart sank.

'Will Granddad be there?' I asked.

'Why wouldn't he be?' she asked, shooting me a sharp glance. 'It's his fucking house. You got a reason you don't want to see him?'

It was as if she was challenging me to say something.

We both knew what she had seen. We both knew that she was well aware that Granddad had abused me many times, and that she had chosen to allow it to continue. By taking me right back there as soon as she had me home, it was as if Mum was showing me how powerful she was.

'I don't want to go,' I said.

'Tough fucking luck. Do you think just because you've been off to your fancy centre for demented kids you can tell me what to do? I don't fucking think so.'

As soon as we got to Grandma's house, she was off.

They were both pleased to see me, but as Grandma hugged me Mum said, 'Come on then, Mum. I've had a really stressful time – let's go to the shops.'

'Oh, I don't know, Jennifer,' said Grandma. 'I want to see our Sophie.'

'She'll still be here when we get back,' said Mum. 'Let's have a day going round the charity shops.'

It was what Grandma loved to do more than anything.

'What d'you think?' she asked Granddad, as I clung on to her skirt, sending out silent prayers that she wouldn't go.

'Treat yourselves!' he said, opening his wallet. 'I'll look after young Sophie here – I haven't seen her for ages. My, you've put on a bit of weight, haven't you?' he leered. 'You're looking grand.'

I pulled away from Grandma and from his lecherous eyes, and locked myself in the bathroom.

'Christ, she's obsessed with pissing, that child,' I could hear Mum say.

They went out a few minutes later and I knew it would all come to a head. There was no way he would let me hide all day, no way he wouldn't extract his pound of flesh from me given that I'd avoided him for three weeks.

I heard him pottering around before coming to stand outside the bathroom door.

'That's them off, Sophie,' he said cheerily. 'Fine to come out now.'

Did he really think I was hiding from them? Did he really think all I wanted was to be alone with him? Maybe he could delude himself that way, I didn't know – perhaps he had actually convinced himself that we were having a relationship that I enjoyed. I know now that there are paedophiles who enjoy the terror and pain of the children they abuse, but I also know that there are those who don't see what they're doing as wrong; they try to make themselves believe that it is a relationship. Was Granddad one of those? That would make sense in a way because, otherwise, why did he go on about the bad men he had locked up when he was a prison guard? The bad men who touched children were something he always went on about and yet he was one of them – did he not see that?

I knew there was nothing I could do to stop this happening; as was the case so often, I just wanted to get it over with. I was well aware now that Granddad was obsessed with oral sex; that was what he always wanted, so when he called out, 'Come on, Sophie, come to my room,' I gave in. I unlocked the door, followed him and did what he wanted.

There was no point in thinking I could resist it. This was my life and there was always someone in charge of me.

Afterwards, he told me he'd missed me and said, 'Don't

worry – everything'll be fine now,' as if this was where I wanted to be, rather than anywhere else.

When Grandma and Mum came back, another decision had been made without my knowledge.

'You're staying here tonight,' said Mum. 'A sleepover – give me a break.'

She'd been without me for three weeks and she already needed a break! Grandma gave me a cuddle and I consoled myself with the fact that there would be no beatings that night, and, as I had already done what Granddad wanted, I would be spared that.

Mum didn't hang around for long. She went off with the bags of things Grandma had bought for her, relieved to have offloaded one of her children for the night. I heard her leave while I was in the living room watching telly. She'd been in the kitchen with Grandma for most of the time since they got back from the shops and, when I heard the door slam, I realized with a heavy heart that she wasn't even going to bother to say goodbye to me.

Later, I got ready for bed (there were always nightclothes and a change of things at Grandma's house for all of us as we were there that often) and snuggled up on the sofa beside Grandma. It was still quite light out when Granddad said, 'You know what, I think I'll treat Sophie to a little drive.'

I'd thought he was quiet because I'd already done what he wanted and there was nothing else to bother me for, but his 'little drives' only ever meant one thing – more sex. It simply hadn't occurred to me that he had been sitting there all that time working out how to get me alone to do it all over again.

'That'd be lovely, wouldn't it?' said Grandma to me. 'Oh, your granddad has missed you so much, Sophie. He talks about you all the time when you're not here – it's special to have someone love you so much, isn't it? You're a very lucky girl.'

'I don't want to go, Grandma,' I said.

'Nonsense – it's no trouble. Off you go, get your coat on and go with Granddad.'

He smiled at me and raised his eyebrows. I hated when he did that, as if we were colluding together.

'That's right, Sophie – let's go have fun.'

He drove me to the woods, his favourite place for outdoor 'fun'. I was so sick of him and so sick of myself that I didn't even wait for him to ask, I just did what he wanted as soon as we were in a spot far away from any chance of someone passing by.

Afterwards, he said to me, 'Will you take your clothes off, Sophie?'

'What?' I snapped. 'I thought we were done.'

'I just want to look at you – go on, take your clothes off.'

I switched my brain off and did it. I removed every stitch I had on as he leered at every inch of my body. I hoped and prayed that someone would see us, but I knew they wouldn't, no one ever did and he always got away with it.

Once he had finished touching himself as he looked at me, we drove back. He did speak to me on the drive, but it all washed over me; there was nothing I wanted to hear. When we got back, Grandma had made supper. I took in snatches of what she was saying – *lovely girl, such a good*

Granddad, fun, special times. It was all shit, but I didn't even have the energy to answer her.

I went to bed that night wondering if they had all had enough of me yet – had Mum hit me enough, had Grand-dad abused me enough to make up for the three weeks I was away?

Some time over the next six months, Dad disappeared again for a while. It was only when I saw my records that I discovered he had been given a suspended sentence and probation order for fraud. That report says that he pre-sented as:

> . . . a 'gentle' man who is caring and concerned for the well-being of his children. There has been a long history of marital tensions, which have caused several separations and frequent suspicions and misunderstandings about this couple. The estate they live on has a high level of delinquency, vandalism and social problems.

I wonder whether his run-in with the law calmed Dad for a bit. He wasn't imprisoned, but he did go off. It amazes me, though, that, yet again, no one saw the truth of the matter. Dad – caring and gentle? My parents – misunder-stood? The only thing that was misunderstood about them was that they were ever thought of as fit to raise three children.

Over the next year or so, nothing really changed. Lots of people were in our lives, watching us and writing reports, but little altered for me. Apart from one thing, one horrible, confusing, bewildering thing. I started get-ting sexual feelings when Granddad was abusing me. I couldn't think of anything worse. From the first time he had shown me the naked cards, he had always wanted to know how I was feeling and if I liked it. I'd never felt anything at that stage and couldn't imagine that I ever would, but, my body was now betraying me. Even when a child is abused, their body eventually matures and with that maturity comes a whole host of feelings and sensations. The shock of feeling something sexual in a situation of abuse is appalling, but it can happen.

If anyone is reading this and has been abused, they may very well know what I mean. They will know the horror of thinking your body has turned against you – how, you think, is it possible to feel good things when you are being violated? What is important to remember is that you aren't aroused by the abuse itself, you are simply responding physically to what your body is experiencing without the context of the illegal acts which are going on.

I'd also like to say that, if any abusers are reading this, you cannot ever justify what you do by saying that sometimes the abused child enjoys it. They NEVER want it. They only want it to stop. You are doing this against their will even if you have conditioned and groomed them to appear as if they do want it. You are raping, sodomizing and violating them each time, and you know it.

The guilt that comes from having a physical response to abuse is almost overwhelming, and I'm damaged by it to this day. At that age, I was just so confused. I started going to the woods myself and taking my clothes off. I showed myself to people as they went past, but, thankfully, never to anyone like my granddad who would have acted on it. Everyone just walked on, no doubt thinking it was a childish prank rather than a cry for help. That became a habit for me for a while. It chills me to the bone to think of that now.

My mother seemed to be able to manipulate everyone. *Manipulative.* It's no surprise that this is a label I was given in every care setting that ever hosted me – I'd learned from an expert. It was as if they just went through the motions of logging meetings that never happened, letters telling her that they had been at the house when she was out, more letters telling her they'd try again, more meetings saying they hadn't seen her for a while. It's not surprising to me that even now children fall through the net. It was bad enough thirty years ago with so many departments involved, but now it's even worse. When I hear cases of poor children like little Baby P, I wonder how close I was to becoming a headline. Mum did her best to bring that about, I feel. In one file from 1981 it states that she simply sent a letter asking that some of the meetings stop completely and that others be changed from weekly to monthly. Unbelievably, a social work letter confirmed this at her request and ended, 'Good luck'.

That happened not very long after I'd been in the assessment centre, so you would think that I would still be under very close supervision, but, actually, it had all fizzled away. I was hardly ever there when social workers or health visitors did call round – if they were let in at all. Mum would lock me in my room, threatening me with all sorts if I made any noise, or make sure I was at Grandma's house. I wonder why the authorities thought this was all fine. I'm sure they were very busy, but what was there in my case that made them all think that the promiscuous, manipulative child who had been taken away for three weeks was now perfectly safe? After all, more than one file states that there was a belief I was at no risk of harm. If what I went through constitutes 'no risk of harm', I dread to think what some children experience.

I was so very damaged, but it took forever for there to be any decisive action taken over my future. In 1982 there was a letter to a child-abuse co-ordinator emphasizing that meetings were informal and not full investigations, but something must have happened to change that because only a month later there was an internal memo stating that there were concerns I was being 'used' by my family. That was an understatement, but there was no suggestion anywhere – and never was – that my granddad was sexually abusing me.

In December 1982, ten days before Christmas, a full care order was given for me. It wasn't before time. I was ten years old, and though so many social workers had been involved in my life for so long none seemed willing to actually see what was going on. I was admitted for more assessment on Christmas Eve.

The Department of Social Service report to the Juvenile Court of that date says:

The above-mentioned girl was admitted to the assessment centre having been made subject to an Interim Care Order for irregular school attendance.

Reading my reports, I'm never too sure whether truancy was the only thing that bothered the authorities or whether they used that as the one thing they could 'get' my mother on. To be honest, I didn't care – as long as they finally got me out of there.

For the next two years, my reports are a list of the various care homes in which I was placed, alongside comments saying 'mother removed child', 'problems at home', 'review required'. The reviews went on, the problems continued and I was passed back and forth as months turned into years. There was talk of me going to a special school and I hated the thought of it – it seemed like a stigma and I didn't want to be labelled again. It turned out to be the best thing that could have happened to me. I had the best two years of my life that far there – and the best thing of all was that it was too far away for my mum to visit me very often as she didn't drive.

It came about through a wonderful teacher called Miss Burnett. I was still desperately latching on to every female teacher there was, looking for attention and love, and Miss Burnett was perfect for me. She was beautiful, with long straight blonde hair, pale skin and blue eyes. I also loved that she had a red coat, my favourite colour. She had a lovely tone with me. Actually, she had a lovely tone with all the children, but I liked to tell myself that she had a soft spot for me.

One day in the assessment centre she came to see me. That always made me happy.

'So, Sophie,' she said gently, 'what do you think of going to a new school and staying there, sleeping there, instead of here?'

I wasn't too sure. The assessment centre was all right really, and I wasn't keen on more change. However, I trusted Miss Burnett and was happy to listen to what she had to propose. When she spoke, it was like listening to a story.

'Shall I tell you a bit more?' she asked. 'Well, it's a huge house in the countryside. It's a perfect place, with lots of lovely children who I'm sure would enjoy meeting a little girl like you. They all get taught there, but they also all go on lots of outings and activities. There's a park in the grounds and so much to do; I'm sure you'd love it, Sophie, but it's up to you.'

I have no idea whether that last bit was true, but Miss Burnett always made it sound as if you were important too and that your opinions mattered. However, there was only one question I needed the answer to.

'Is it far away?' I asked.

She looked a bit worried.

'Well, yes, I'm afraid it is quite far away,' she replied, unable to lie to me as she was such an honest person.

'Far away from here?'

'Yes – rather far.'

'Great,' I told her. 'I'll go. I want to go.'

If it was far away, Mum couldn't get there, or at least she couldn't get there easily. She'd been messing things up since I got to the assessment centre. She'd come and get me, take me home, leave me with Granddad and Grandma, he'd abuse me, she'd collect me again, beat the shit out of me and then I'd go back to the assessment centre in a never-ending cycle of despair.

I had to wait until the following week for a visit to take place and I was sick with nerves the whole time. Mum wasn't scheduled to visit me over that time, but she kept to her own schedule, so if the mood took her she was perfectly capable of just turning up unannounced. I dreaded that happening. Miss Burnett told me that the new place was called Marlow Hall and it was all I thought about. Marlow Hall. Marlow Hall. I could imagine myself there. *Hello – my name's Sophie Gilmore and I live at Marlow Hall.* I could be a new person at Marlow Hall. I could be the Sophie I'd always wanted to be.

Rushing through my head every minute of every day was the thought, *What if it doesn't happen?* Each time the bell rang or the phone trilled, I thought it was Mum coming to get me. When that didn't happen, I wondered if Miss Burnett would work out that I was a horrible little girl, dirty, disgusting and filthy, and realize that I wasn't actually fit to be at a nice school after all.

But the time passed and nothing bad happened.

On the day she told me she would, at the time she had arranged, Miss Burnett came for me. Beautiful, lovely, reliable, kind Miss Burnett. We got into her little blue Mini and went for a long, long car ride. Marlow Hall was way out in the sticks, just as she'd promised, and just as I needed it to be. With every minute that passed, I could feel myself getting further away from Mum. It was as if I could see her in the mirror behind me, getting smaller and smaller, disappearing from my life like a bad dream.

As soon as I saw the signs for Marlow Hall, I relaxed. There was no way my mum could get here. The school was set in a mansion in perfect grounds. It was massive, surrounded by trees and fields. There were slides, a see-saw, swings. I had the notion there was freedom within my grasp even before I went into the school building.

Miss Burnett squeezed my hand as we walked in together. Waiting for us was the headmaster, Mr Trent. He was really tall and I had to bend my head back to see him smiling at me. He shook hands with me and said, 'I bet you're hungry.'

We went to the dining room and I got the shock of my life. It was huge, with paintings of past pupils hanging from the walls and tables groaning under the weight of food. If Hogwarts had been invented back then, I'd have thought I was in the middle of a Harry Potter tale! All the children were sitting at different tables. It was noisy, with lots of laughter and chat, but not rowdy at all, just happy.

I remember that I had a rah-rah dress on, which was very fashionable at the time, although far too short and flirty really. When I sat down, one of the girls said, 'I like your dress,' and the others all started agreeing. It was a lovely welcome. The food was lamb with mint sauce, my favourite, and when the kitchen staff came to take our plates away, I already felt settled. Everyone was around me once the plates had gone and I had my first baptism.

'Right, right,' said one of the older boys. 'Let's get the important stuff out of the way first.'

My heart sank. Was there going to be some horrible initiation? I thought so; this place had seemed too good to be true.

'Sophie! Sophie! Sophie!' they all started chanting.

My stomach was churning. What was it going to be? I told myself I could take anything and waited.

'Quiet!' shouted one of the girls beside me. 'Sophie, this is very important – think long and hard before you answer, OK?'

I nodded.

'OK – follow your heart . . . Elvis or Shakin' Stevens?'

I didn't have to think long and hard.

'Shakey of course!' I squealed.

The place was in uproar. The boys threw their heads on the table in mock agony, the girls held my arms and cheered their victory. My new friends were all shouting, 'We beat you, we beat you!' to the boys.

It was lovely. I felt so happy and so safe.

After lunch, Miss Burnett came with Mr Trent and they showed me round the grounds. I could hardly believe that I was being allowed to walk there, never mind being considered as a resident. It was all so clean and everything smelled nice. I wanted to live there immediately.

'Can I stay?' I asked Miss Burnett.

'No, Sophie, I'm sorry,' she said. 'This was just a trial – we needed to see if you liked it here.'

How could I not like it? It was perfect, so far removed from all that I was used to, but I had to wait for two weeks while they sorted 'things' out. I suspect that meant dealing with Mum. When I was given the news that I could go, that Marlow Hall was waiting for me, I was elated. Finally, I was in charge of my own life. Marlow Hall was full of opportunities and I just hoped that I hadn't been damaged too much to take every last one of them.

Chapter 13

Back to square one

The recommendations are:
To remain in residential care;
To be allowed to stay at home for one night on
alternate weekends and for up to two weeks at
school holidays at the discretion of field and
residential staff;
To recommend to the Education Review that a
place be sought at special school; if her domestic/
family life were stable she might cope with normal
school but it isn't.
Given the need for much first-hand contact with
her mother and the occasional unease about the
two boys at home, responsibility for the case
transferred to Area Office. When at home, it is said
by Sophie that there is often a deterioration in her
relationship with her mother, causing numerous
arguments and unhappiness.
Report after one month in care
Social work files 4325G/
Sophie Gilmore

I should have guessed there would be a drama before I got there, though. I'd been for a home visit before moving to Marlow Hall. Mum and Dad were at each other constantly from the moment I got back. I'm not sure if he was hitting her more than usual, I don't actually think so, but there seemed to be an edge to it all that hadn't been there before.

The first night I was home, shut up in my room and wishing that I was already at Marlow Hall, Mum came flying into my room and said, 'Right – get your things, we're off.'

My stomach lurched. Granddad. We were going there, I assumed.

'Does Grandma know we're coming?' I asked. I always tried to ask questions indirectly, knowing I'd get a clout if Mum thought I was being 'cheeky'. Most things were cheeky in her eyes.

'No, we're fucking not. He's hit me for the last fucking time, the mental bastard – we're off to the women's refuge,' she said.

'I can't go there!' I told her.

'Why not? Too good for it, are you?' Mum replied.

That was a laugh, given my home environment.

'No – but Miss Burnett's coming for me in two days. I'm going to Marlow Hall; she won't know where to find me.'

'Marlow Hall?' she laughed. 'Lady Muck, aren't you? The only place you're going is with me. Come on.'

Mum, Mark, Alex and I all traipsed off to the refuge, where we were given a tiny room. It was horrible, but safe. Mum was really unsettled as it wasn't clean enough for her, and she took it out on me as much as she could. She had to be quieter and more discreet than usual, given that we were in a domestic violence shelter, but she still managed to get a few punches in and blame me for everything.

The next day, we had to see the woman who was warden of the refuge. She took all our details and said we were safe. She had no idea of what was really going on, and Mum was just using her as she used everyone. We had to stay out of the refuge for some of the day, so when we were walking the streets, I wandered off. I was used to making phone calls and I'd taken some coins from Mum's purse, not caring if she found out. Getting to Marlow Hall was all that mattered, so I phoned Miss Burnett and told her where I was.

The next day, as planned, she turned up. I heard her voice at the door to our room, and she sounded like an angel to me.

As she called, 'Sophie – are you in there, dear?' Mum put her fingers to her lips and indicated that I was to keep quiet. It was a ridiculous ploy given that the refuge had to be very careful over where everyone was, with the result that they had a policy whereby you had to sign in and out. They would know Miss Burnett was safe, and they would have told her that we were definitely in the room.

Miss Burnett kept saying my name, and Mum kept whispering to shut up, but, finally, finally I found my voice.

'I'm in here, Miss Burnett!' I shouted. 'I'm in here!' Mum kicked me but I didn't care. 'Get me out – please get me out!' I called.

She must have gone to get the warden, because, minutes later, the door opened. Miss Burnett, very calmly, said to Mum, 'Hello, Mrs Gilmore – as you know, today's the day Sophie starts a very exciting stage of her life. I'm sure that you'll want to wish her well.'

Mum simply shrugged and turned her back on both of us.

As I sat in Miss Burnett's little blue Mini, I breathed the biggest sigh of relief in the world. I'd got out. I didn't know what the consequences would be with Mum, but I was heading for Marlow Hall. I looked out of the window and felt the weight of my mother lifting off me. I knew she was too skint and too lazy to make the trip, and that these were more pertinent reasons than her not being able to drive. I just prayed to God that she would leave me alone, forget about me even. That would be for the best.

I was so happy and so welcomed in that school. I went swimming, did outdoor pursuits, canoeing, rock climbing, abseiling. We went walking in the woods and we picked berries to take back so Cook could make pies. I found that I could sing, and they were always getting me to sing solo. I was on a float for the local carnival. I was happy every day. I didn't want to see Mum at all; I just wanted to stay there forever.

She came the odd time, first with some guy she'd met, then the next time she said she'd divorced Dad – just like that! 'I'm getting married again,' she said. 'Must need my fucking head examined.' I didn't miss her and I didn't care.

I latched on to Mrs Jackson more than most. She was pretty and always praised me even when I didn't do well. At 'normal' school, the teacher had thrown things at me because I looked out the window when I couldn't do the work but Mrs Jackson was always lovely to everyone – she had time for us all. They all did. We had discos nearly every night and I found I loved music more than anything; it got me through. We were typical girls – typical friends then enemies – at that school, just like normal kids. We'd hold hands, then hate each other the next day. It was all as it should be, but I found that I was very easily influenced by boys. I was a bugger. They were always having to watch me; I was promiscuous, not in terms of having sex as such, but always fondling and kissing when I got a chance. It was how I was. I'd even chat up the workmen when they came in. Within days of being at Marlow Hall, I got my first boyfriend. I was only eleven.

The problem was that the authorities wanted to 'fix' my relationship with Mum instead of writing it off. They kept letting me go home, and that was a big mistake. I hated going home, obviously. I was a two-week boarder for months. I went to school on Monday and stayed there until the following week's Friday, then go home for the weekend. At first, I went to a different children's home at weekends, then they decided everything was fine and I went to Mum's. Eventually, they made me a weekly boarder and I went back to the children's home on some weekends, and spent some at Mum's from Saturday till Sunday and it was then I'd see Granddad. Mum was beating me up all that time. I'd go home and be exhausted when I got back to Marlow Hall as I'd had a weekend of beatings from her and abuse from Granddad. She'd keep changing her mind about whether I could be fostered or not, and messed with me so much. The two-week boarding went so fast and I would count down how long till I had to see her again. I'd start playing up at the end of the two weeks. I think it was such a bad idea to keep that going on, to keep taking me back to her; I hated it. No one made the decision to say 'You're not seeing your daughter and if you do it has to be under supervision.' Someone needed to do that.

One time when I was at home, Mum was out and I was trying to relax before the onslaught she would undoubtedly unleash on me when she got home. I was sitting in the living room when Mark and Alex came in.

They settled themselves down on the sofa beside me, and I got the sense that they'd been having a conversation before they came through.

'Sophie,' Mark said eventually, 'we've got something we need to do.'

'Have you?' I answered absent-mindedly. 'What's that then?'

They shoved each other a bit and whispered. I could hear a few comments such as 'No, you do it', and 'No, you said you would'.

'Right,' I announced. 'Spit it out. What's going on?'

Mark looked at Alex before he spoke.

'Well . . .' he said haltingly. 'It's Granddad.'

'What about Granddad?' I asked.

The boys looked at each other again.

'He says . . . he says . . . he wants us to touch you,' stammered Mark.

'He WHAT?' I shouted.

'He wants us to touch you – it's what he told us to do. He said you wouldn't mind,' said little Alex.

A wave of fear washed over me and I couldn't quite believe that they were reaching their hands out. I slapped them away.

'No! Of course you can't touch me!' I screamed. 'What in God's name do you think you're doing? Tell me exactly what he said.'

'Just that we should touch you. That you'd like it. That it would be fine,' said Mark.

All the things Granddad had told me – and now he wanted my little brothers to do what he did to me. Was there no end to this man's evil perversions? I tried to stay calm and ask them the question I didn't really want to know the answer to.

'Mark, Alex – I need you to tell me . . . does Granddad touch you?'

They nodded.

'Does he touch you in private places?'

They nodded again.

'Has he been doing it for a while?'

Dear God – more nods.

I took a deep breath.

'Are we not going to be allowed to touch you, Sophie?' asked Alex.

'No – no, you're not,' I said.

They looked at each other.

'What will we tell Granddad?' asked Mark. 'Will he be cross?'

'Tell him that he needs to keep his hands off you or I'll cut them off,' I said.

The boys both giggled. They seemed completely unperturbed and thought it was funny that I was threatening a grown-up; worryingly, they also seemed to accept what Granddad was doing to them and what he had asked them to do to me as perfectly normal.

I went back after that weekend with a heavy heart. How on Earth could I protect them when I wasn't even there? Trust wasn't something I could feel for adults at all. There was no way I could tell anyone – if I did, Mum would find a way to make it all my fault, and, anyway, I trusted no one, not really, not deeply. So, who would believe me, who could I tell? Not Mum – and the social workers had me marked down as trouble. If the boys denied it, I would be labelled as a liar too. I just had to pray that my brothers would go back to him and repeat my threats, hoping that he would take it as a warning and stop. I had genuinely never thought he was touching them. I had thought he was only interested in making my life a misery. All the time, I thought I only had to protect Mark and Alex from Mum, but it was so much worse than I'd imagined.

Mum resented me being away as she couldn't control me, so she took it out on me when I was back. On my twelfth birthday I was given sixteen pounds in total by all the different people at Marlow Hall. That was a lot of money in those days. When I came home that weekend, I just wanted a bit of peace. I had an idea: I thought, *If I give Mum all my money, she'll be happy.*

When I got in, she didn't even mention my birthday. I waited for a bit then told her.

'Right,' she said, 'I've got you nothing, so if you're angling for a present, you'll be disappointed.'

'It doesn't matter,' I lied. 'I got money from Marlow Hall. Look . . .' I showed her the sixteen pounds. 'Do you want it?' I asked. 'You can have it if you want it.'

She screwed her eyes up at me.

'Yeah?' she said.

'Yeah,' I smiled.

'Great.' With that, she snatched the cash from my hand and left the room.

I hoped for a calm weekend, but there was no chance; by the next day she was at it with men again. It was as if I never did learn what she was like.

Before I left for Marlow Hall that weekend – my birthday weekend – she said, 'Sophie – your birthday . . .'

'Yes?' I said, a little bit of hope rising in my heart.

'You borrowed a couple of quid from me last month – I guess you don't have to pay it back. Happy birthday.'

It was always like going back to square one. Often, as soon as I was dropped off by the school minibus, she'd whisk me round to Grandma's house. Granddad hadn't stopped abusing me – why would he? He'd got away with it for so long that he must have felt invincible.

Once, when he was trying to make me give him oral sex, I was foolish enough to say no.

'Why not?' he asked. 'It'll be fine, it'll be all right.'

'No,' I told him. 'I've got a boyfriend now,' I said proudly.

'Oh have you?' he laughed. 'Well, I bet he's a dirty little

fellow, isn't he? Always touching you? Always putting his fingers up inside you? Always wanting you to kiss his thing?'

No, I wanted to shout, *that's you, that's your perverted behaviour.*

'Is he big?' Granddad asked. 'Is he as big as me?'

I wouldn't answer him. He disgusted me as always, but I had, inadvertently, given him another stick to beat me with.

'I wonder what your mother would say if she knew you had a little boyfriend, going where he shouldn't,' he taunted. 'Do you know what I think? I think she'd tell that fancy school of yours and I think you'd get kicked out. Your dirty little boyfriend too, I shouldn't wonder. Now, if you know what's good for you, you'll do what you're here for.'

So I did.

On the next visit, he smelled smoke on me. I was smoking heavily by then, despite my age, as there was always someone at Marlow Hall with fags. He blackmailed me with that too. He would always start by saying he would tell Mum, then quickly realized she couldn't care less – all I was bothered about was whether I'd get to stay at Marlow Hall, so he used that against me instead, threatening to tell them and get me kicked out. He had me where he wanted me, and where he'd had me for years.

I had my first bleed round about then. It only lasted for a few days then I didn't get my proper period until I was thirteen, but it gave me an idea. Next time Granddad was at me, I said, 'You can't touch me; I've got my period now.'

'What, now? Right this minute?' he asked.

'Yeah. Yeah, I have,' I said proudly.

He thought about it for a moment. 'Doesn't matter,' he said, 'your mouth's fine.'

How could the authorities possibly know all that? They never asked, and, despite the few veiled concerns about sexual abuse raised in the files, there was never any investigation. Another report said:

> Sophie has been spending weekends at home and always returns saying that things have gone well. It is difficult to ascertain how true this is as both mother and daughter collude on many matters. There does not appear to be any major problem arising from Sophie's home leave.

They were wrong, wrong, wrong. We didn't collude. I was terrified of her and would say anything that she wanted me to say; that wasn't collusion, that was fear. So many people seemed completely blind to my mother and I was sick of it. Things would be logged such as:

> Sophie is grossly over-familiar towards all members of staff.

Without anyone really asking WHY?

In November 1983, when I was eleven, rubbing their hands in self-congratulation, the co-ordinator of the Child Abuse Section wrote to the Department of Social Services:

> I am pleased to inform you that the above child's name was removed from the Child Abuse Register by the Divisional Review Committee in November 1983.

It must have been nice for them to able to tick a box. *Sophie Gilmore – removed from the child abuse register.* And what was happening before, during and after this? I was being touched by my granddad, forced to give him oral sex, having to touch him, being shown lewd pictures, being put in danger by my mother, being beaten by my mother, being neglected and hated and mistreated as I had been for as long as I could remember.

By 1984 I was in a pattern of spending weekdays at the young people's home, while weekends and holidays were at Mum's. By the summer of that year, I was home full-time on a trial and my records state that my home circumstances were more stable. That isn't true – things were never stable, but I was getting older and I was finding my voice, even if I still didn't fully trust any adult.

By the end of that year, we were re-housed and that made things a bit better in a superficial sense, but Mum never changed – there was nothing that could be done about how she treated me and about the way she lived her life. I didn't really want to be at home at all, but the social workers were always trying to look for positives, always trying to see ways they could get me back there full-time. They finally listened to me and I went back to the pattern of weekdays with Mum, coupled with weekends and holidays in the home. My notes only say 'problems at home'.

That's an understatement.

A letter from spring that year from the observant headmaster at Marlow Hall, Mr Trent, to Miss Smithson at the Department of Education tried to ring more warning bells. In it Mr Trent said:

Further to our many telephone conversations of recent weeks, I can now bring to light some quite disturbing facts learned after going to fetch Sophie to school last week. As you know, Mrs Gilmore was not at home when we called, but was at the end of the street with Sophie somewhere nearby. After some time, Mrs Gilmore walked towards her home with her three children. She appeared to be somewhat agitated and was having a conversation with a man who happened to be passing as Mrs Gilmore came to the minibus. A houseparent at the school got out and had a conversation with Mrs Gilmore, during which Mrs Gilmore asked 'Who could look after her boys tonight?' The houseparent talked Mrs Gilmore into allowing Sophie to come back to school, but she was adamant that she wished Sophie to come home for the weekend. She tried to arrange for the man who was listening to all this to send his son for Sophie on Friday evening. At this point, we closed the minibus door and drove Sophie back to school.

During the journey, Sophie appeared to be relieved for this to have happened. She told us that she had been asleep in bed with her mother until 3.15 p.m. that afternoon, and that she did not get to bed until after 2.00 a.m. She also told us that, quote, 'Loads of times I stay at home with the boys while my mum goes into town to sleep with her boyfriend.' Sophie had a long conversation with me during the evening and stated quite forcibly that she does not want to go home. I went some way towards preparing her for not spending weekends at home with her mother for some time.

I have instructed my deputy, who is working some

weekends, to allow Mrs Gilmore to take Sophie if she should come to school anytime, but to then discuss this matter with yourself, with a view to the police being asked to return Sophie to school.

Further to this letter, Mrs Gilmore visited the school five evenings ago, the night after the above took place, and again the following evening. On the first evening, Sophie was out of school and Mrs Gilmore went away quite quickly. On the next evening, I talked to her for one and a half hours and plainly put it to her that I would let her take Sophie home at 4.00 p.m. on that day, but would then call the police to get her back.

Sophie has been to see me again, and, using my experiences of these matters, I have no course to disbelieve her, she says that she has drunk 'bleach, Silver Dip and washing-up liquid in the past.'

Could that man possibly have made things any clearer? There is so much in that letter – and so much was still ignored. That he believed me is a wonderful thing; I only wish I had known it was the case back then as I could never trust anyone who was good to me – this is so sad in retrospect as there were good people around me, like Miss Burnett, but I guess I was just too damaged to take that leap of faith and confide in them. I wish I had – I really do.

However, the paperwork was piling up thick and fast.

In December 1984 Mum moved with all three of us to another new house with her new husband. I didn't like her new man, and always suspected she was just trying to get back at Dad who had, by now, moved to Wales. There must have been some concern about the behaviour of both of them towards me, and the files state:

> Mrs Gilmore and her husband profess distress at Sophie's removal from home; they insist that they did not abuse her in any way, while acknowledging that her behaviour was difficult. Nonetheless, they accepted the recommendations [that I moved out for longer periods] with some equanimity. Sophie's progress is undermined by family discord. There is no evidence of the ebullient and friendly girl that was evident when last in residential care. At home, there has been recent discord. The girl has complained of harsh treatment.

About six months later, when I was twelve and a half, there is a medical report from the General Infirmary that says:

> . . . mother hit Sophie with a stick on Sunday x 2. The stick was about 2 feet long and struck her on the leg and right upper outer chest. This Tuesday mother hit Sophie on the head with her hand, and this is apparently not unusual. Skin has old mottled bruises approx 5-7 days old. Repeated chastisement appears likely to continue.

This letter was from a lecturer in paediatrics who had examined me, and was sent to the NSPCC, another hospital, three people in Social Services and the Social Work Department. They all knew that despite Mum's insistence that she didn't hit me, she did.

It all went on in the same fashion for the next three years. My life was very predictable – and it was always crap if Mum was involved. By 1985 my reports were littered with indicators that I was still a very troubled young girl. I was living at Marlow Hall by then and from the spring of 1985, it all sounds the same:

Sophie went to meet a boyfriend without permission.

Sophie is sly and devious.

According to others she is asking strangers for money and cigarettes.

Sophie performed her favourite trick this morning and tucked her wet sheet under the mattress.

Sophie has been wandering around in other rooms in her bra and also had hidden two pairs of dirty pants under mattress.

Matron rang to see if Sophie had a brown/rust dress – if so, it belongs to another girl. (Sophie said she had brought it from home.) Also, a black jacket was taken from her and when her bed at school had been moved there was a pair of dirty pants with a gold ring belonging to a member of staff that had been missing since Easter. Sophie denies any knowledge of ring or pants. Matron will try to keep an eye on Sophie and search her, and we will have to see that she doesn't bring anything in here.

Matron rang to say that Sophie had blackmailed a boy into giving her money and another into giving her a tape.

Matron rang again re Sophie – it seems children at school who are found to have cigs and matches are saying that Sophie has provided them. Sophie in tears because X's toy elephant was found in Sophie's locker and she said she hadn't taken it.

I was a bad girl; they all thought it, and now I was about to play up to it more than ever.

Chapter 14

Is this really happening?

Sophie gave initial disclosure of sexual abuse,
which was fully consistent with that of her
brother's disclosures taken earlier today. She also
named the perpetrator as being her grandfather.
Sophie was obviously distressed and very
concerned about her brothers. She expressed
feelings of relief that we now knew and agreed to
give a full statement to the police. I requested that
Sophie be interviewed by a female member of the
police unit. Sophie also expressed this wish.
Social work files 4325G/

Sophie Gilmore

Although his attempts at penetrative sex had thankfully
stopped, Granddad was still trying to get me to touch him
and give him oral sex whenever he saw me. That was less
often than it had been, but even once would have been
too much. I was getting more rebellious and I would tell
him to 'Fuck off' more often than not, but it didn't seem
to matter. He just laughed at me and threatened to tell

Mum that he knew I was smoking or sleeping around. He was right on both counts, but I wonder now why I thought she would care. I think that I must have been so locked into this horrible hold he had over me that I couldn't see the truth. I could have stopped it.

I would tell him to piss off, but Granddad would say, 'Don't you talk to me like that, young lady – I'll tell your mother.'

'Go on then,' I'd retort, but as soon as he made any move to do so, I'd take it all back. 'I'm sorry, Granddad – don't tell her.'

'All right then,' he'd say, smiling. 'It'll be fine.'

I'd do what he wanted me to do because sometimes, too many times, it was better to do that quickly than to get battered by my mum all evening when we got home. I think he knew what she was like with me. He had me over a barrel.

Finally, something did click.

Finally, I'd had enough.

At some point when I was sixteen, I was given permission to smoke by the residential home. This meant that one of Granddad's controls over me had gone. I was staying over at his house – Mum had dumped me there as soon as I'd got back – and I was wearing a nightie. I was sitting as far away from him as I could, but Grandma was in the kitchen and he reached over and just grabbed my breast, bold as brass. He was leering and licking his lips, like the stereotypical old pervert he was.

'Get the fuck off me,' I hissed.

'Don't you swear at me,' he said as if he had done nothing wrong.

'Get. Your. Fucking. Hand. Off. Me. Now,' I told him. 'If you don't, I'll punch you. I will.'

I didn't even know where the words were coming from, but he didn't stop. He tried to touch my leg next, running his hands up my thigh as far up as he could. Out of nowhere, I whacked him on the chest, really hard. Within seconds, Grandma walked in with a big plate of home-made chips and doorstep bread. She looked at us in a very odd way. Granddad was flustered and panting, because it was a hard punch. He was red in the face and shocked.

'Are you all right?' she asked me.

I nodded.

'You?' she asked him.

'Fine, fine, Grace – no worries, no worries here,' he lied.

She pottered off, stopping once at the door to look at us again.

As soon as she had gone, I spoke to him.

'If you fucking touch me again, you'll regret it. I prom-ise you.'

He never did.

He never touched me after that.

In the past, I would have thought that would have been half my worries over, but getting Granddad out of my life wasn't the start of a new, wonderful life. I was taken into care again in the autumn of 1986 and placed back in the residential home Marlow Hall. Soon, I started running away from there too and they were having to report my absconding to the police. I felt lost. Things were chang-ing. I was getting older and knew that being in care wasn't an option any more. Running away was a way to get attention and getting attention was something that comforted me, since it was all I knew. I had felt comfortable in the previous places – when one place closed for the holidays or couldn't take me, I would go to the other, but they were placing different conditions and restrictions on me now that I was older. For example, they always wanted me back by 11 p.m. and my automatic reaction to any rule was to break it, or at least try to. I had found a job by that time, and was travelling there and back each day, which was seen as important for my maturity. I may have appeared to be growing up, but, inside, I was still in turmoil.

I had met a boy called Gavin and was madly in love. It was always all or nothing with me. All it had taken was for him to wolf whistle at me, and I was lost. I liked the attention; perhaps I was more like my mother than I wanted, because even although I was already going out with another boy then, Gavin told me that was over and I was his. We hadn't been together for long when I decided that I was going to run away from the home. Gavin asked me where I was going and when I mentioned a flat I could use, he said it was too dangerous and to leave it to him.

The next day I told him that I had definitely decided to go, whether or not he approved of my choice.

'You can stay with me,' he said.

I liked the idea, but I told him that I wouldn't sleep with him. I wanted my own bed. He made me a makeshift one, but it was no use – I had sex with him that night; I didn't know any other way to act really. We were inseparable from that moment; it was a very passionate, intense relationship and I loved him so much. I thought there was no one like him, but I was completely blinkered as he was a waste of space.

I put all my eggs in one basket with Gavin. He did love me to start with but it didn't last and he was soon sleeping around. I used sex to keep him. I'd do anything. Oral, threesomes with a girl, threesomes with a boy, the boy for him, the boy for me, the girl for him, the girl for me; it didn't matter. Sex was the only currency I understood and I had zero self-respect.

I told him I was pregnant even though I knew I wasn't. He told my mum and it all kicked off at the home. Gavin wasn't making me happy but I couldn't bear to let him go.

In 1987 my files says that I had been caught 'flaunting' myself at boys at the window. I'd been caught doing that before, but, for me, it was always a sign that I was very upset and seeking attention the only way I knew how – through my body.

On Valentine's Day 1988 I took an overdose of imipramine, and was admitted to hospital in a coma in the early hours of the morning. I remember being taken out of my room by the ambulance men, then nothing until I woke up in hospital, lying on my back. When I opened my eyes, I saw a big plastic jug at the side of me.

What the hell's that? I thought. I looked around and the doctor in the room noticed I was awake. I realized where I was but asked him, 'Why am I here?'

He started to explain what I had done, and that the jug was full of what they'd taken out of me, but I had to interrupt him; he'd completely misunderstood my question.

'No – I mean . . . why am I here? I'm supposed to be dead. Why didn't it work?'

It hit me that I'd even got suicide wrong.

I tried twice again, both times with paracetamol, but when it didn't work I tried to tell myself it was for a reason. I was meant to stay here a bit longer.

I remained in hospital for a week, not only because I needed to have psychiatric assessments, but also because there was nowhere for me to go. There were staffing problems at Marlow Hall, and my mum wouldn't take me back. My social worker collected me on my release. Four days after I got out, I was allowed to go home for the weekend.

The report from my social worker states:

> Sophie in an angry mood. I spent all the interview encouraging and allowing her the space to get some of this anger out. Some was clearly directed at me, at Marlow Hall and her mother, but at least now not at herself.

I was given approval to go on the Pill in April 1988 as they all knew I was sleeping with Gavin, but that was the least of my worries. The psychiatrist said in his report of that time:

> I am deeply concerned with the effect that her home environment has on her emotional development.

There is a copy in my file entitled Review of Child in Care a month later. It says:

> Sophie has gone through a difficult period since the last review. She was admitted to the general infirmary and is

to see a doctor tomorrow. Her relationship with her family continues to have highs and lows – at present the relationship between Sophie and her mother is quite good. In school Sophie presents few problems – she puts very little effort into basic subjects but works hard with keenness and confidence in non-academic subjects. She had been accepted on to a one-year course at college in September designed for students who have missed out on schooling. Her mother did not want to say anything in the review and did not send in a report. It is known that there has been, and may still be, 'problems' in the home. She is satisfied that Sophie is being cared for appropriately and wants her to remain here.

There is part of the report attached that records my answers to questions. In it, I say that I 'keep having bad tempers and sulking'. It also says that I feel better going back to the home after home visits. 'My mother is very special to me.' She was – but they probed no deeper, just taking that as evidence of normal love.

In summary, her relationship with her family continues to be one of falling in and out. She told the review that she did not want to go and live with her mum and wanted to be fostered. From observations of Sophie's relationship with her mother during the review setting, there were some indications that Sophie was 'frightened' of her mother.

The review agreed and recommended:

1. Sophie should remain at Marlow Hall.

2. There should be no restriction on Sophie's wish should she express it to visit her mum either for a day or for overnight stays.

3. The social worker would make an application to the Home Finding Unit with a view to a long-term foster home being found for Sophie.

In September 1988 I genuinely thought that I was pregnant – I'd been trying for a while in order to get out of care. I wanted a baby so badly, someone to love and someone to love me. I told my care worker that I was pregnant, but I had no idea. Every month I would hope that my period would be late. This time it was a false alarm. My file states that:

> . . . on the 11th September, Sophie's mother phoned to inform me that Sophie was pregnant by her boyfriend, Gavin. About two months. I rang Gavin who confirmed what she had said and that it had been planned so they could get a flat.

I did want a baby, but sex was very muddled up for me and I had played the pregnancy card with Gavin before. Because of the abuse, I did think that sex was all I was good for. All I wanted was to be better than whoever the man I was with had slept with before. That was all that mattered to me. The only thing that gave me pride was when someone said I was great in bed. I wanted to give the best sex, be the wildest, the most up for it, the most experimental. I never wanted to be a woman who had a headache or who said they didn't fancy it that night. I was always available, always ready – and always put on a bloody good show of acting as if I was having the time of my life, even when I was screaming inside.

My relationship with Gavin lasted until I was eighteen. One day he said I was the best he'd ever had – but walked away. I couldn't understand it. If I was so good, why had he slept with all those other girls?

I wouldn't accept it. I stalked him. I behaved terribly as it seemed like the end of the world to me. I'd given him sex, I'd given him great sex – so why had he left? As a teenager, I'd sleep with anyone – and always wanted to know if I was the best they'd ever had. Even now, with my husband of twenty years, I'll never say no, I'll never say I don't want to. Even though he knows me inside out, I still only value that relationship on the basis of whether he gets all the sex he wants from me. Sometimes I ache for it to be different. I sometimes want him to hold me and know that sex is not on the agenda, but then I always think I should be up for it – always offering, always being the sex object because that's all I know to offer men, because it's all I was. I know he loves me, and I know he would do anything for me, but he can't change what I am inside.

I wish I could wash my brain. I wish I could take it out and give it a damn good scrub, getting rid of all the memories and bad things. I'd be a different person if I could do that.

With my husband, Peter, it is a loving relationship but it was hard to start with. He would say to me, 'Why are you doing these things, Sophie? You don't need to prove yourself to me.'

He told me he loved me, but I didn't believe him for a long time.

In fact, even now, sometimes, I can't believe it. I'm not educated, I haven't achieved anything, so why else would he be with me? I just want him to love me for me and I know it goes back to those years as a child and as a teenager when it was all I had to barter with, all I had for people to notice me.

One night, when I got back to Marlow Hall, the supervisor called to me.

'Sophie, love – can you come into the office please?'

I thought quickly. What had I done wrong? Nothing new, nothing out of the ordinary.

I followed her through, ready to deny whatever she accused me of.

'You need to sit down, love,' she said gently.

'I've done nothing,' I began.

'I know, I know – but you do need to sit down,' she went on. 'I had a phone call today from your social worker.'

'I've done nothing,' I repeated.

'Sophie – just listen, please. Your brothers have made an allegation.'

An allegation?

What allegation?

'They've told their social worker that your granddad has been sexually abusing them,' she said. I thought I was going to faint. They'd *told*? Really? 'They've also said that he has sexually abused you, Sophie.'

I couldn't believe what I was hearing. I couldn't believe

they'd told someone, and that they'd told about me too. I sat there for ages, unable to say or do anything.

I had to check, so I asked her again.

'They've told their social worker he's been touching me?'

'Yes, yes they have,' she confirmed.

I ran upstairs to my bedroom and slammed the door.

An hour later, someone knocked on it. It was the police but I ignored them, then heard my mother's voice telling me to stop being so stupid and open up.

'No! Get away!' I screamed. 'I'm not opening it, so just leave me alone!'

They came in anyway.

I was so confused. I had thought for so long that I wanted people to know, but now that they did, I wanted to turn back the clock. They'd blame me. They'd all know what I'd done. They'd know I was dirty and damaged.

As soon as the police came in, I denied it all.

'He didn't touch me,' I said.

'For fuck's sake, Sophie,' said Mum, 'you know he did – just tell the truth.'

Why the hell was she supporting me now? Why did she want me to tell the truth after all these years of knowing herself?

I followed the police down to their car and they took me to the station.

There was a lovely policewoman there called Dorothy, who I still remember. She was so patient as I gave my statements, one after another. I told her everything and it felt like a weight was being lifted. I didn't want to hide it any more.

Mark, Alex and I were all interviewed separately and not allowed to speak to one another about it. In total, I gave twenty-nine statements. They needed to know what was distinctive about him, and they got it all – his smell, birthmarks, the colour of his pubic hair, every nasty little detail.

At the end of it all, Dorothy asked me what I wanted to happen.

'Do you want to see him locked up?' she questioned.

'Yes,' I whispered. 'Yes, I want him to pay.'

My brothers disagreed. They tried to retract everything but it was too late. However, because I was the only one who wanted Granddad prosecuted, I felt as if I was on the outside again.

Grandma obviously found out what was going on and she called me at the home as soon as Granddad was taken in for questioning. I was so glad to hear her voice.

'Grandma!' I cried.

'Shut up,' she said, with a tone of voice I'd never heard before. 'Just shut up. I have no idea why you are saying these horrible things, Sophie, but listen to me – I don't believe a word of it. You're a nasty, lying little girl and I never want to speak to you again.'

'But, Grandma – it's all true, he did it all, I swear he did!' I wept.

'You're a liar – you've always been a liar. I should have listened to your mother about you. Know this, Sophie – he, your granddad, is my husband and I will stand by him. You're nothing to me. He'll be found innocent and everyone will know what a deceitful little liar you are. This will all blow up in your face and you'll be shamed by your lies, you mark my words.'

I wept that night, I wept like I had never wept before, for I loved my grandma and she was all that had kept me going through those years; but she was wrong. I wasn't a liar and the court believed me, not him. The trial happened quickly. He pleaded guilty to everything, so no one had to give evidence in court and he was found guilty on all counts.

Guilty of indecent assault against a minor.

Guilty of sexual abuse.

Guilty of attempted rape.

Granddad was given eighteen months and sent to the very prison where he had worked as a guard, the very prison where he told me other prisoners hated the men who did bad things to children. He was out in twelve months for good behaviour, moving to a different area so that no one knew him, and Grandma did indeed stand by him all along. I never saw him or my grandma again.

I was still off the rails. I'd thought that if he was found guilty, I'd feel free, believed and a new person. It didn't work that way. I was still me. I started abusing solvents, I bullied and I cheated, I even tried prostitution.

Then . . .

Then I met Peter.

I was at a party when he walked into my life. I thought he was gorgeous from the moment I set eyes on him – he was very broad and muscular, in a white T-shirt and black trousers. My way of flirting was to push and shove a lad;

so I did a lot of that in the kitchen with Peter. It was as if he could see right through me from the second we met. He kissed me that night and we went back to his flat, where, for the first time ever, I felt loved by a man.

That was it.

I moved in a week later and we've never been apart since that day.

He was my rock from the moment I met him. Peter has a calmness and is a deep thinker; I needed someone to balance me out and he's always been able to do that. I told him everything from the start. He'd heard so many nasty things about me and it was important to put the record straight. He listened and didn't judge me. I fell in love with him and, to my complete astonishment, he loved me back. It's never stopped surprising me, but, from that instant, my world changed.

I was loved and I could now get ready to fly.

Chapter 15

The best mummy in the world

There are weighty opinions (mostly from doctors) that we should abandon thoughts of Sophie having a future with her family: the inconsistency of the family, the recent suspicion of physical abuse, the hints of possible sexual abuse all contributing. Views about 'finding a nice family' are, in my view, unrealistic. The mother would oppose it   that would not, of itself, inhibit us, but the girl could not cope with the implicit rejection of her mother at present. Neither Sophie nor her mother could be expected to cope with the conflicts of loyalty that could attend a placement.

Social work files 4325G/

Sophie Gilmore

Peter and I had only been together for a short time when our lives changed forever.

I'd always thought I was unable to have children. I thought that the things done to me by my granddad might have caused some damage. He'd always had his fingers inside me, and he had poked and touched me since I was so very small, that I believed some physical harm had been done. I also felt so dirty and so ashamed of my past that I thought, even if there were no physical consequences, I would be punished somehow, and that I would never be able to carry and hold a baby of my own. It hurt me deep inside, but I almost thought I deserved it. When you spend your childhood being told that you are nasty and unwanted, that you can't be loved because there is something wrong with you, that never disappears. As much as I yearned for a baby, I never thought I would be blessed.

In fact, when Peter and I spent our first night together, he asked if I was on the Pill.

'No, but don't worry,' I replied. 'I can't have children.'

I believed what I was saying. Even when I had wanted a baby of my own years earlier, it hadn't happened. I'd never used contraception at any point with any of my boyfriends, and I knew the problem was with me, because some of them already had kids. It was me – I was rotten to the core.

A couple of weeks after Peter and I got together, I had breakthrough bleeding, not a full period but enough to make me think that was me done for that month. But then, over the next few days, I had weird stretching feelings in my tummy and I was going to the loo all the time. I was so exhausted that I felt I could sleep standing up, so I went to the hospital to find out what was wrong with me.

'Is there any chance you could be pregnant?' the nurse asked.

'None whatsoever,' I told her as Peter held my hand, worried about why I had got so tired and so weak all of a sudden. 'I can't have kids,' I said, repeating what I told everyone, and what I truly believed.

'Well, we'll do a test just to check,' she said. 'We need to rule everything out.'

Peter left the room to get some lunch, and by the time he came back, I'd had the news I never expected.

'You're pregnant,' the nurse said, coming back in to see me.

'What?' I asked. 'No – I can't be, I can't be.'

'There's no doubt about it,' the nurse told me. 'You're going to have a baby. It'll all be fine, we can get someone to talk to you about your options. Don't panic.'

She took my denial as worry or a sign that I didn't want a baby, but it wasn't that at all. I was desperate for this to be true, aching with every part of me to be told that I really was pregnant, but I couldn't believe that something could go so right for me.

When Peter came back in, I was still in shock, but grinning from ear to ear.

'I'm pregnant,' I told him quietly. 'Pregnant.'

'But you said . . .' he began.

I started crying. There was no way I would get rid of this baby, I would keep it no matter what, but I realized it was so much to ask of Peter. He had only just turned sixteen, we barely knew each other, and we didn't have two pennies to our names. I'd do this alone if I had to.

'Why are you crying, Sophie?' he asked. 'This is brilliant! This is just the most amazing thing – I'm going to be a dad!'

He never left my side from that moment onwards. Our love for each other had been instant, and we loved our baby from the second we knew I was pregnant. I was given a scan that day and found out I was nine weeks gone. I remember the sonographer saying to me, 'Look, can you see that little sac?' When I said I could, she told me, 'That's your baby,' and I felt like screaming with joy.

Peter and I went back to the flat, where I had moved in with him only a week after we first met, and held each other tightly. It was a happy time, but we knew it would be hard. What kept me going was the instant connection I had with my unborn baby. I was in love from the start.

Real life was not so straightforward. A couple of months after I found out I was pregnant, things were getting more and more difficult. Neither Peter nor I were working – there were few jobs around at that time if you were unskilled, uneducated and from a bad area that came with its own reputation. On top of that, the tiredness that I'd felt from the start of the pregnancy hadn't lessened. I was constantly exhausted. We had practically no money at all, so moved in with Peter's mum. She had disliked me from the outset, believing I wasn't good enough for her boy, and she was always shouting at me for falling asleep when we lived there. Peter was out looking for a job all day, every day, whereas I could barely lift my head up. My body felt as if I'd run a marathon and Peter's mum had no sympathy. She wouldn't believe it was the pregnancy as she'd sailed through hers, she just thought I was lazy. Even when it was discovered that

I was dangerously anaemic, she couldn't care less and said she'd had enough of us, throwing me and Peter on to the streets when I was about six months pregnant.

The pair of us trudged into town, carrying what few possessions we had, and went to the Social Services department. It was a strange moment for me, raised as I'd been to never volunteer any information to the authorities, but expecting them to always provide what Mum demanded. In the event, we did tell them exactly what was going on in our lives and they offered us accommodation – in separate hostels. I couldn't bear the thought of being away from Peter and started sobbing, sure that we'd be kept apart for so long that I would end up losing him, no matter how many promises he made. Once again, I was plunged back into my childhood, feeling that I didn't deserve to be loved and that any happiness out there wasn't for me.

The woman who had suggested the separate emergency accommodation was really sympathetic and then said that we could get a room together in a hostel, but it would be pretty dire, and that the separate rooms would be much better. I told her that I didn't care, as long as we were together.

It was just as she'd said. There was a tiny room for us with hard bunk beds and a single wardrobe with one chest of drawers in a corner. You were expected to be out all day, and, as we had no money, we'd walk the streets in all weathers, with my tummy getting bigger and the baby kicking. I spoke to my child all the time. I told him or her that it wouldn't matter if we had nothing material, we had love. I vowed to be the best mother I could, despite having nothing to base that on. I would do my best and I would always support my child.

At that time, the government gave pregnant women on benefits a one-hundred-pound maternity grant. With it, I had to get everything for my baby. I bought a second-hand buggy at a car boot sale. I found a charity shop that sold babygrows and tiny cardigans for ten pence each, and I cleared them out. There was a sterilizing unit for three pounds too, which I snapped up. I didn't care that it was all second-hand; I'd do whatever I needed to do. Fancy prams and posh outfits meant nothing to me; the baby wouldn't care where his or her clothes came from as long as they were clean and warm. I washed everything and folded it carefully into the chest of drawers, taking out tiny little outfits every so often and wondering if I would ever really have my own baby to cuddle.

Every day, when we left the hostel, we had to sign out, then sign back in when we returned. One day, when we went to the desk to collect our key again, I could see that there was a note stuck on the board with my name on it, just beside the key.

'What's that?' I asked the supervisor of the hostel.

'Oh,' she said, smiling, 'it's good news, Sophie – there was a phone call earlier. You and Peter have a flat!'

It couldn't have come at a better time. I was eight months pregnant and we just wanted to build a nest for our forthcoming arrival.

'Don't get your hopes up,' the supervisor said as we rushed upstairs to pack our things. 'It won't be up to much.'

She was wrong. It was perfect. We moved into the

little flat and couldn't have been happier. All I wanted was Peter and the baby, so this was a bonus. It was a tiny two-bedroomed place above a shopping centre and I saved up until we could afford a Moses basket from one of the shops there. I would stare at it in the window every day. I was so proud on the day that I paid for it and took it home. I had high blood pressure by this time, and when I went into labour two weeks early, the doctors were worried. It was a slow labour, and after contractions for more than twenty-four hours, I was still only two centimetres dilated. It went on and on, but, finally, with Peter beside me as he had been all along, our beautiful baby was born.

Our little boy, Darren, was born with his big blue eyes open, looking at me as if he already recognized his mum. I was in love. My heart felt like it would burst and the tiredness didn't even register.

It had happened!

I had a baby; I was a mother.

I looked at him that night and thought, *You're mine, I gave birth to you.* It was an amazing feeling, as if all I had been through in my life was worthwhile now that I had Darren. The midwives had put him in a baby nightie while I was still recovering from the epidural, and I thought, *Oh no, that's not what I planned for you to wear at all!*

I dragged myself out of bed and dressed him in an all-in-one that had yellow bunnies on it and a matching cardigan. It had all been bought for pennies, but I felt the richest woman in the world. I took the baby — my baby — over to the rocking chair in my room and opened up my big pink dressing gown. I put Darren on my bare skin and held him there all night. I made such promises.

I'll protect you.

I'll look after you.

I'll love you.

I'll never let anyone hurt you.

Twenty-one years later, I hope I've kept those promises. I still love my baby boy as much as I did the first day I held him.

Peter, Darren and I were a little family straight away. We went home to the flat and I felt as if it was us against the world. I still do.

Eighteen months later, I had my second son, Andrew. Three years after that, along came Jack, then another three years brought Harry. Peter and I were as much in love as ever. Our four boys meant so much to us, and we were an absolutely devoted family. People would say to me, 'You're so lucky to have a family like that.' Throwaway comments from people who have no idea – but they can trigger such memories. I'm not lucky – I've worked at it. I could have fallen into my mother's patterns. I could have gone from man to man. I could have wallowed in misery, saying that I'd been dealt an unfair hand. Instead, I've fought for years. Fought to build a happy home, maintain a faithful relationship and rise against my past.

Most importantly, I have been the mother I never had. I've done it all myself. I had no role model, I had no one showing me the right way. I knew I would never hurt or neglect my children, and I'm so proud that I have raised such wonderful people.

Six years ago, I discovered I was pregnant again. None

of my previous pregnancies had been easy as I was always prone to high blood pressure, anaemia and pre-eclampsia, but I would never have considered not going ahead. With this one, there was always a little voice in the back of my mind saying, *I wonder if I'll get a girl.*

Although I loved my boys dearly and wouldn't change them for the world, I yearned for a daughter. I suppose, in some ways, I wanted to give a little girl the childhood I'd never had. Throughout the pregnancy I kept my dreams to myself and Peter. Whenever anyone asked, I'd say I didn't mind, but I wanted a girl so much.

When she was born, when the midwife said, 'Congratulations, you've just had a little girl!' I couldn't believe it.

'Hello, Daisy,' I said to her, smiling through my tears. 'I've waited so long for you, my darling – but it's all been worth it, it really has.'

We've barely been apart since that day. I lost lots of blood when I delivered her, and the doctors said I mustn't have any more children as my body has basically given up and I might not make it through next time. I barely listened. None of it mattered. I had my little girl and our family is complete.

Telling my story has brought so many things back – not just the memories of the abuse, but every step of my journey. I hope that some of the people I have met along the way read this book. They might not know who they're reading about, they might not remember the little girl who wanted to be saved, but if what I've revealed opens their eyes just a little bit, it'll all be worth it.

All those people who thought I was a trouble-maker,

an attention-seeker and manipulative, I want them to know it wasn't my fault – this is why I am the way I am, and this is why I was that way as a child. It still affects me. I want to work with the elderly. I did it before and I want to do it again, but everyone needs staff who can read and write well, and I can't – but how can I begin to explain to strangers why that is? I want to help people and I want to care for them; I have so much love to give but I don't have bits of paper, which seem to be more important. As soon as I need to spell or count, I'm just no good. I feel as if my brain can't handle it, especially maths. I don't know how much of that is from my past too – not just the time I missed at school, but the terror of getting things wrong, which reminds me of what Mum would do to me when I got things wrong as a child.

I also feel that, every time I get a little bit of happiness, it's snatched away. I've had happiness in my life, I know that, but I've never appreciated it or allowed myself to engage with it fully while it was there. Mum always said, 'If I'm not bloody happy, why should you be?' She's still there in my mind, her voice haunting me every day.

I want to feel happiness and joy. I think negatively too much and I overthink; I concentrate on the worst-case scenario. Even if it never happens, I make myself ready for it because that's how I was taught to survive. I don't know how to be happy, I can't let myself go. I want to be able to but I've never known where to start. Maybe this book will help, maybe it will be the start of a new Sophie.

Even while writing it, I've thought the publishers would change their mind, the ghostwriter would stop believing me, and everyone would dump me. I thought they would all turn round and tell me how rubbish I am. I am full of self-loathing but I also know that there must be so many people who feel just like me, because there are millions of abuse survivors out there. If telling my story makes one person realize that it wasn't their fault, it was worth it.

I've always wanted to tell my story but I worried that without a good education I wouldn't be able to. When I found someone who could help, I then worried that no one would believe me. When it was pointed out to me that there were records, that Granddad had been convicted and that there was lots of evidence, I still worried. I've always worried. The memories are always there and I sometimes do feel that I can't get past my demons. I can be fine for months, then I'll see something on TV or see a headline and it all comes back. People talk about abuse much more these days and that's a good thing, but it does mean that there can be triggers where you least expect them. I've had counselling, but I had to stop because the therapist kept crying when I told her my story.

I hate my granddad and I hate what he did to me, but I hate my mother even more.

More than anything, Daisy's innocence has affected me. Watching her has brought home to me how much was stolen from my childhood. She's such a girly girl and I love to indulge her. She's inquisitive and clever, she wants to wear my perfume, my jewellery, my shoes. I'm giving her the childhood I wanted; I'm the mother I wanted to have when I was little.

To be honest, although I always wanted a baby to love, I was scared as hell when I first found out I was pregnant, but, once they were born, it all came so naturally to me. I guess I'd been watching for years to see how it shouldn't be done – all I had to do was the opposite to my own mother. I grew up when I became a mother. I suppose that seems odd because all the social-work reports about me say that I was old before my time, that I never had a chance to be a child, and, yet, I feel as if I only really became a full person when I was a woman. I also got a chance through my kids to have the childhood I'd never been allowed to experience. I would dress up with them, have sweets for breakfast on birthdays, cuddle when one of them had nightmares, play games at all hours of the day, never say no to any fun they wanted because I could never deprive them of anything. I was allowed nothing, happiness was denied to me, so I was damned sure that would never happen to my little ones.

I get flashbacks all the time. Only recently, I was in the park with Daisy, pushing her on the swings.

'You're the best mummy in the world,' she said to me.

I smiled and kissed her as she swung back to me, but then, in the middle of the happy moment, I got a chill. I remember myself at that age. In play parks. Alone. For hours every day, asking random strangers to push me because I had no one who cared. They never did. They blanked me, never asking why a small child was on her own for so long, ignoring safety rules to talk to people she didn't know, begging for attention. I paint the smile on my face again when I'm with the kids, but sometimes there is so much pain in my heart when I remember that lost little girl who just wanted someone to make the decision, to take her away from it all.

Earlier this year, I had taken Daisy to school and was on my way back to catch the bus. I heard a whimpering noise and looked down a side street, only to see a little girl about the age of my daughter, maybe a year younger.

'Are you all right?' I asked gently, walking towards her. 'Where's your mummy?'

The child didn't answer me, but I could see that she had been crying as the tears streaked her face and she was still breathing in that gasping way children do when they're trying to be brave. The little one was nicely dressed but obviously cold.

'Where do you live?' I asked.

After asking a few times, the girl pointed down the street and I could see that one of the doors was ajar. I went down to it, knocked and called to see if anyone was in, holding the little girl's hand all the time.

No one came until I had shouted about four or five times, then a woman came to the door, looking like she had just got out of bed.

'I was upstairs,' she snapped. 'What do you want?'

I told her that her daughter was cold and on the street, but she didn't seem to care.

'I'm not her bloody mother,' she said, grabbing the little one's hand and dragging her inside. 'I'm looking after her and she's nothing but trouble.'

She slammed the door in my face and I went home. I was shaking while I was on the bus. A tear-stained little girl being called 'trouble' and neglected – it was too close to what I had been through. I couldn't stop thinking about it and felt awful. I looked out for her again when I went to collect Daisy, but there was no sign of the child. As I held my own daughter's hand, I knew I couldn't leave this be. What if that girl was praying for someone to help her? What if she felt she was invisible and no one would ever come to her aid?

I settled Daisy down with a DVD and some snacks, then called Social Services. I reported it all, giving the address and even leaving my name, despite still being scared of the authorities after my own childhood. I don't know what happened, but when I told friends, they all congratulated me and said I was an 'angel'. That's the problem, I think. I'm not an angel, I didn't do anything amazing. I did what we should all do, I looked out for a child. The very fact that people thought this was worth commenting on and out of the ordinary is shocking. Why don't we all look out for all the children around us? Why aren't the abusers and neglectful parents the terrified ones? Why isn't our society caring for the most isolated and vulnerable ones amongst us?

I think that I have a good heart and I do care a great deal. I wear my heart on my sleeve and I'm not ashamed of that. I guess that was one of the reasons I decided to write this book. Sometimes I just want to forget everything, but if there is the slightest chance that telling my story can help someone, then it's worth it. If anyone is reading this and doesn't know what to do about their own experience, I'd say, tell someone. Don't hold it in, because it will eat away at you. Sometimes I think, *I wish I'd told*. Then I remember: I did. Mum knew Granddad was abusing me, and I had told her that Dad was too. I gave my statements, Granddad was convicted – so why do I still feel that I've let myself down? I don't feel fixed and I still wish someone had heard.

What I try to do is concentrate on what I have, not what can't be changed. I feel rich with what I've got. I know I'm adored. One of my boys starts university soon, and they all have career plans. Daisy has the most idyllic childhood a little girl could have. She is given her innocence, never forced to grow up too soon, always allowed to be her own person.

All I can do is what I know – keep being a good mum, keep being a good person. I've forgiven my dad. Mum is another matter. She knew exactly what she was doing. I told her when I was pregnant with my first baby, hoping, as always, that she would be the mother I needed. She let me down, yet again. She turned her face to the wall and didn't say a word. I have seen her a few times over the years but there is no relationship there. She still talks to me as if I'm just someone she knows, never as her daughter. If I ever mention the past, she tells me to get over it, says that I'm fine, so what am I dragging all that up for? She'll never be a mother to me, and all I can do is try to stop her affecting me any more than she already has.

Grandma and Granddad are both dead. I miss her so much and I wish she had believed me. When I was little, she always said that I'd get her rings when she passed. That never happened. Mum got them and taunted me as much as she could.

'Told you!' she said, waving her fingers at me. 'Told you all along that it was me she loved!'

I still love my brothers dearly and am close to them. I

know that they don't want to talk about things, but they have supported me telling my side of the story and that means a lot.

I suppose the only ones who are left are the people who could have taken me out of that situation. How do I feel about them? Times were different then, people didn't talk about child abuse, but those were professionals – they did have an awareness or, at least, they should have done. I find it hard to forgive them. I think that I was so close to being a statistic, a child whose name was in the headlines, whose face was on front pages, and I do think it took them far too long to do anything about it. Too often, when I read stories of children who have not been rescued, there are many similarities with my own story – a manipulative mother, missed appointments, departments not communicating, everyone thinking that someone else was dealing with the problem; while the 'problem' has a name and a face and cries real tears every night while she prays for someone to notice her.

That was me – I was that little girl, that 'problem'.

If you're that little girl too, or that little boy, or you know someone who is, please don't stay silent. It is so important that we all speak out against these terrible people who steal childhoods. Do what you can. Look at every child in your life and ask – *Are they OK? Do they need anything? What can I do?* Every child is the responsibility of every one of us – don't walk by, don't close your eyes, because you never know if it might be me.

I'm still out there.

Millions of children like me are surviving, just getting through, praying it will all end.

I still wish that someone will help me, I still need fixing, but, more than anything, I want every child to be saved.

After you've read this book, hold your children tight. Tell them that you love them, that they're special. It doesn't matter if you have no money, if you have a small house, if you can't afford the latest gadgets and designer labels. Just love them.

Please – just love them. xx

Acknowledgements

My husband, Peter, has always been there for me, through the highs and the lows. He has seen how I have been treated by those who should have loved me and he has given me everything I have needed to get through. I was a bit of a wild child when we got together, but his calmness has done me so much good. I have always needed someone like him and I'm eternally glad that we found each other. Thank you, Peter, for seeing me as a person, for seeing me for who I am and accepting it all, and for loving me, no matter what.

To my five lovely children – I am so very proud of all of you. I know that I was meant to survive because I now know your love. If I had given up, none of you would be here. The world is a better place because you are all here. Darren, Alex, Jack, Harry and Daisy – always remember that your mother loves you all so much and please promise to make something of your lives; then I'll know all the hard work and struggles over the years were worth every minute.

As I have had to use a pseudonym and change all names to tell my story, it's an odd feeling to be thanking people for all they have done for me but not using their real names – I hope you all see yourselves in these words!

My best friend, Rachel, has been there for me for more than ten years. She is there for a coffee and a chat, no matter what is going on in my life. I have always respected her wise words and know that she is a true friend who I can trust. Thanks, Rachel – I love you.

I have a friend who I have known for twenty-three years so I hope she recognizes herself through that. Nicola – we have had our ups and downs, but you are someone I could never have *not* had in my life. Whenever I am feeling low or unhappy, I can always rely on you to cheer me up. We have shared so many memories together; I will never forget them.

I'd also like to thank my social worker, Caroline Davies, who took me away from it all. Mum had hit me over the head with a sweeping brush the night before and I genuinely thought I would never get away from the hell that was my home life. Miss Davies came the next day and took me to safety.

Another positive presence in my life was Miss Burnett, the teacher who knew that I needed extra help as I had missed out on so much schooling and socialization with other children and adults who knew how to behave appropriately. It was Miss Burnett who reassured me that everything would be all right. While I was at Marlow Hall, I really felt that I could be a child for the first time and that meant a lot.

Finally, I'd like to thank my ghostwriter Linda Watson-Brown so much. She has worked alongside me to put this book into your hands. Thank you, Linda, for believing in my story and for never giving up on me when you easily could have. It's been a long road but we got there in the end! There's absolutely no one else I would ever have chosen to write this book for me. You made me feel at ease when I poured my heart out to you and I told you things I've never told anyone before, and you have listened and believed every step of the way.

To everyone else involved in this book, who has believed there is a story to tell, thank you — there's a little girl inside me, who will hopefully sleep a lot easier tonight, knowing that her story is out there.

If anyone would like to get in touch with me, then Linda will pass on all emails in confidence if you mail her at *l.wb@stampless.co.uk* I hope that reading my story helps — and I hope that you all get the happy ending you deserve too.

xx

He just wanted a decent book to read ...

Not too much to ask, is it? It was in 1935 when Allen Lane, Managing Director of Bodley Head Publishers, stood on a platform at Exeter railway station looking for something good to read on his journey back to London. His choice was limited to popular magazines and poor-quality paperbacks – the same choice faced every day by the vast majority of readers, few of whom could afford hardbacks. Lane's disappointment and subsequent anger at the range of books generally available led him to found a company – and change the world.

'We believed in the existence in this country of a vast reading public for intelligent books at a low price, and staked everything on it'
Sir Allen Lane, 1902–1970, founder of Penguin Books

The quality paperback had arrived – and not just in bookshops. Lane was adamant that his Penguins should appear in chain stores and tobacconists, and should cost no more than a packet of cigarettes.

Reading habits (and cigarette prices) have changed since 1935, but Penguin still believes in publishing the best books for everybody to enjoy. We still believe that good design costs no more than bad design, and we still believe that quality books published passionately and responsibly make the world a better place.

So wherever you see the little bird – whether it's on a piece of prize-winning literary fiction or a celebrity autobiography, political tour de force or historical masterpiece, a serial-killer thriller, reference book, world classic or a piece of pure escapism – you can bet that it represents the very best that the genre has to offer.

Whatever you like to read – trust Penguin.